WHAT TO DO WITH THE KID WHO ...

Developing Cooperation, Self-Discipline, and Responsibility in the Classroom

Kay Burke

IRI/Skylight Training and Publishing
Arlington Heights, Illinois

What to Do with the Kid Who ...
Developing Cooperation, Self-Discipline, and Responsibility in the Classroom
Sixth Printing

Published by IRI/Skylight Training and Publishing, Inc.
2626 S. Clearbrook Dr.
Arlington Heights, IL 60005
800-348-4474, 847-290-6600
FAX 847-290-6609
irisky@xnet.com
http://www.business1.com/iri_sky/

Editing: Julia E. Noblitt
Book Design: Bruce Leckie
Illustration: David Stockman
Manuscript Input: Donna Ramirez
Production Coordination: Kim Overton, Lisa Stiegman

Library of Congress Catalog Card Number: 92-64102

ISBN 0-932935-42-7

1131E-3-96McN
Item Number 0841

Dedication

This book is dedicated to my husband Frank, my mother Lois, the Brown and Burke families, and the memory of my father, Bob Brown. My family members taught me the importance of maintaining a sense of humor, developing a sense of responsibility, and cooperating with others long before I tried to teach these skills to my own students or tried to write about them in this book.

Acknowledgments

> "I am a part of all that I have met."
>
> —Tennyson

This quote describes how I feel about the thousands of students and teachers with whom I have worked throughout the last 22 years. To teach is to learn, and I have learned from the best educators in Ft. Lauderdale, Florida; Oviedo, Florida; Stone Mountain, Georgia; and Tucker, Georgia, where I have taught in both high school and college. I have also learned a great deal from my friends in cities like Buffalo, New York; Virginia Beach, Virginia; Red Deer, Alberta; Rockford, Illinois; and many other cities where I have trained teachers in cooperative learning and discipline.

I am especially grateful to the teachers from Elgin, Rockford, and Wheeling, Illinois, who were enrolled in the first Field-Based Master's Program sponsored by Saint Xavier University and The IRI Group. These wonderful teachers shared their insights and problems about classroom management, cooperative learning, and student responsibility. It is reassuring to know that so many dedicated professionals are still committed to discovering new ways to motivate students and to enhance learning.

I would also like to thank Jim Bellanca, the executive director of IRI. Jim gave me the opportunity to be a part of his innovative educational team, and he also encouraged me to write this book. His advice, support, knowledge, and judgment have been invaluable.

Words are not enough to express my gratitude to the staff of Skylight Publishing. These creative people always maintain their sense of humor and a sense of calmness amidst deadlines, delays, and "rush orders." Robin Fogarty, Julie Noblitt, Bruce Leckie, David Stockman, Donna Ramirez, Jerry Trueblood, Jamie Bellanca, John Conick, Lisa Stiegman, and Mike Melasi exemplify professionalism.

Lastly, I would like to thank the rest of the IRI staff, who model the cooperative spirit that is threaded throughout all of our courses and seminars. Pat Kalicki, Bruce Williams, Beth Forbes, Mary Jane Bloethner, Amber Palozotto, and Beth Swartz are just a few of the very talented people at IRI who make it all happen every day. We are all in this together, and working cooperatively with a group of dedicated professionals makes the challenge of restructuring education a team effort.

Foreword

Another book on classroom management? discipline? responsibility? Yes! and No! These topics are of genuine interest to educators we have met here at home in the U.S. and as far away as Norway and Australia. From the novice to the seasoned veteran, the critical question is the same: "What do I do with the kid who...?" Teachers share with us their frustrations at the growing number of youngsters who are out of control. In our cooperative learning training programs, the first comment is usually, "Great idea, but what do we do with the kids who...?"

Many discussions with classroom teachers across the United States, Norway, Canada, and Australia have evolved into the contents of this book. Kay Burke, an award-winning teacher of the year, an assistant high school principal, and now a staff developer, leads the way in thinking about how to help classroom teachers best answer the nagging "what do you do...?" question. First, she collected data from her inservice classes about the most annoying and difficult misbehaviors. Next, she worked with the IRI consultant team to classify and evaluate the information. This led to a list of "students who" scenarios that three focus groups of experienced teachers from urban, rural, and suburban schools rank ordered.

The selection process was easy. What proved difficult was coming up with "what to do" answers. The teachers in the focus groups made clear the criteria that they felt would most help in selecting the responses to the misbehaviors. These criteria, coupled with the IRI consultant team's commitment to the values of cooperation, respect, and responsibility, *and* to what the literature on best practices in classroom management says "works," provided a framework.

There are six criteria set by the teacher focus groups:

No quick fixes or magic recipes. Virtually all the teachers felt that there were too many books that promised instant cures. "If I hear another suggestion that all I have to do to change a child's misbehavior is write his name three times on the board or drop some beans in a jar, I will retire. I don't need to be more assertive. I need to find serious solutions to serious problems."

No more expert theories. "I want to know that the person giving me advice has been in a classroom and worked with today's children. I don't need admonitions from a professor who hasn't been in a classroom since graduating from high school."

No wishful thinking. "Let us investigate practical approaches that respond to our children's real needs. My classroom is filled with students who take their lives in their hands just walking to school. Wishing these students had two parents with middle class values is like wishing I could play basketball like Michael Jordan."

A practical problem-solving approach that uses common sense. "I used to be able to say easily to a student, 'If you do a, b will follow.' Those days are long gone. What I need are ways to think about the problems."

A way to motivate students to take responsibility for their own behavior. "I hear a lot said about the power of a student's internal locus of control. Helping my students develop that motivation is a challenge."

A way to encourage students to care for each other. "Life is no longer 'everyone for herself.' My students' survival depends on learning to help support each other."

Kay creates a context and a triple agenda for encouraging all students to become responsible, respectful, and caring students. Kay reviewed both the social and economic conditions that influence students and the "best practice" knowledge that has emerged in the last decade. This review sets the stage for her triple agenda: a threefold synthesis of best practices for the constructive management of students in the *whole classroom,* the *small group,* and the *single student.*

Four groups of experienced and committed classroom teachers and staff developers, more than 300 in all, studied the material, used it in their classrooms, and provided feedback. The result of all this experience and research is a book with these very unique attributes.

1. It was developed *by* teachers and staff developers *for* teachers and staff developers. Not only did they use best-practice research, they made sense of that research through the filters of their own experience.

2. It uses the encouragement work of Driekurs, the quality work of Glasser, the cooperative social skill work of the Johnsons and Cohen, and the caring philosophy of Kohn to filter the model that takes positive discipline into a new domain of application.

3. Its review team of practioners designed a holistic process method that imbeds the values of cooperation, responsibility, caring, and respect into every aspect of the curriculum. In the truest sense, management and instruction are integrated into every niche and corner of the classroom so that students can construct their own rich environment of learning.

4. It does not assume that responsibility, cooperation, and caring just bloom in the classroom. Without reliance on rewards, without turning students into reward junkies, without reliance on punishments and simple recipes to correct misbehavior by heavy-handed authority, the book provides options for making each student a team partner with the teacher—ensuring that all have an equal chance to learn.

What follows contains much of what is familiar to skillful teachers. What is presented is a powerful process which teachers can use with their colleagues to say: "Management issues are not the teacher's fault; with a repertoire of strategies, colleague support, and a problem- solving process built on responsibility and caring, classrooms can be a place for learning the most important lessons of life.

—James A. Bellanca
Chicago, 1992

Table of Contents

PART I
The Rules of the Game

Section One
DISCIPLINE IN THE CLASSROOM

Section Two
TEACHING COOPERATIVE SOCIAL SKILLS

PART II
The Challenges

Section Three
STUDENTS WHO HAVE TROUBLE ACCEPTING RESPONSIBILITY

Introduction

WHAT ARE THE ISSUES?

If half of all students are not working because they perceive that school will not satisfy their needs, we have to attend to the fact that a major institution in our society—perhaps the one on which we spend the most money—follows a theory that does not address itself to the needs of more than half of its clients.
(Glasser, cited in Gough, 1987, p. 657)

Glasser's quote reflects the frustration that many students in schools today are experiencing. Students live in an age of information overload, an emphasis on standardized test scores, societal drug use, physical and mental abuse, increasing violence, and economic insecurity. In their search for identity and sometimes survival, they look to schools as a respite from the realities of life. Too often, however, concerns about covering the curriculum, raising standardized test scores, and maintaining discipline and control take most of the attention of educators. In an effort to keep control, teachers fall back on a structured routine that includes lecturing to students, assigning questions at the end of the chapters, requiring students to fill out ditto worksheets for homework, and giving an end-of-the-chapter test on Friday.

Regardless of the teaching methods used, approximately fifty percent of the students in school today will "play the game." They will take notes during the lectures, they will do their homework, and they will study for their tests. These students are among the "satisfied" group Glasser describes. They value school; they value learning; their parents support their values; and they feel school meets their academic and social needs. But what about the other fifty percent? What about the large group of students who do not want to sit still all day and listen to teachers talk *at* them about things that have no relevance to their lives? Many students choose *not* to sit by passively. They choose instead to fight back and make teachers notice them, usually by demonstrating negative behavior. No amount of coercion is going to make these students learn. As Glasser suggests, "the old theory, 'we can make 'em work; all we have to do is get tough,' has never produced intellectual effort in the history of the world, and it certainly won't work in this situation" (as cited in Gough, 1987, p. 657).

A "new" theory, control theory, is based on the fact that everyone is internally motivated by needs that are built into people's biological structure. Glasser explains the following:

> From birth we *must* struggle—we have no choice—to try to survive and to try to find some love, some power, some fun, and some freedom. To the extent that we can satisfy these needs on a regular basis, we gain effective control of our lives. (cited in Gough, 1987, p. 658)

Making students work by "getting tough" is not the answer. The "pour and store" philosophy of the teacher pouring knowledge into the empty heads of the students is becoming almost as obsolete as the mimeograph machine. A new era of cooperative learning, positive interaction, self-esteem, student empowerment, and student responsibility has replaced the era of competitive classrooms and traditional lock-step discipline. Glasser's idea of control theory in the classroom, Curwin and Mendler's discipline with dignity, Kohn's case against competition, and the work by the Johnsons, Bellanca, and Fogarty describing the importance of teaching social skills are becoming the cornerstones for learning in the twenty-first century.

Restructuring

Education will change more in the 1990s than it has changed in the last century. Read almost any newspaper or periodical or watch television news to see the information explosion in education. *America 2000,* the *SCANS Report,* restructuring, integrated curricula, nongraded schools, de-tracking, yearlong schools, authentic assessment, inclusion (mainstreaming), multicultural education, cooperative learning, and merit pay are just a few of the issues in education. The President and the nation's governors in the *America 2000* program are offering one million dollars to each of the 535 congressional districts throughout the United States to come up with their own educational program that will work for their students and community. Legislators are frustrated because their educational policies are just not working; therefore, they have given school districts the mandate to explore other options.

Canada is also exploring these issues. The ministry of education in British Columbia has developed *Year 2000: A Framework for Learning* that addresses the dropout rate and other important problems in the educational system. Anthony J. Brummet, Minister of Education, reports that "while our system has served the learners of British Columbia well in the past, it needs to change to reflect changing societal conditions" (Educational Programs Department, 1989, p. v).

The Royal Commission on Education found that the school system served college-bound students very well, but that it was not serving students who chose not to attend college. It also found that the seeds of the dropout problems may be sown in elementary years, when students do not see the relevance of the curriculum and demonstrate a lack of interest in and engagement with school learning activities (Educational Programs Department, 1989, p. 2).

Cooperative Learning

Research shows that innovative changes in education should include the cooperative learning educational model. This model incorporates team work, higher-order thinking, social skills, leadership roles, and active learning in the classroom. The research of the Johnsons, Slavin, Kagan, Sharan and Sharan, Bellanca, Fogarty, and others has encouraged teachers to meet the challenges of teaching all students.

Cooperative learning helps teachers make learning more meaningful and motivating; it also encourages students to become interactive learners and to develop the social skills necessary for life. A caring and cooperative classroom, however, does not necessarily eliminate the traditional types of behavior problems.

Except for those who live in deepest poverty, the psychological needs—love, power, freedom, and fun—take precedence over the survival needs, which most of us are able to satisfy. All our lives, we search for ways to satisfy our needs for love, belonging, caring, sharing, and cooperation. If a student feels no sense of belonging in school, no sense of being involved in caring and concern, that child will pay little attention to academic subjects. Instead, he or she will engage in a desperate search for friendship, for acceptance. The child may become a behavioral problem, in the hope of attracting attention. (Glasser as cited in Gough, 1987, p. 657)

The importance of establishing a caring, cooperative classroom so that students can attain the acceptance they so desperately need cannot be emphasized enough.

The Caring Classroom

Bellanca (1991) sees the establishment of a caring classroom as a significant teaching challenge because of three problems. The first problem involves the "put-down, competitive culture of most schools and most communities" (p. viii). Bellanca also feels that students' attitudes will take time to change because they are immersed in the negativity they see on television and hear from their peers. The final problem involves finding the time to teach social skills in an already crowded curriculum. Bellanca sees the explicit teaching of social skills in a cooperative learning classroom as part of the solution to those problems.

Glasser (1990) envisions a Quality School of the future. His school would be free of discipline problems because there would be no coercion; therefore, students would neither be punished nor artificially rewarded. In the Quality School, students would not have to learn "nonsense" facts that have no use in the real world. They would instead do work that they agree has quality and relevance. Finally, students in the Quality School would evaluate their own work to see if they have learned the important lessons in life (in Brantigan and McElliott, 1991). The discipline problems that plague most schools today could be reduced if students were allowed to participate in decisions regarding their education and allowed to assess their own progress.

As long as students' needs for love, belonging, caring, and sharing are not met, they will continue to act out these frustrations. The following chapters deal with how to establish procedures, rules, and consequences in the cooperative classroom; how to teach specific social skills so students are aware of what behaviors are expected of them; how to solicit student feedback to establish classroom group rules; and how to handle individual problems as they arise. The effective cooperative learning teacher can also learn how to become an effective classroom manager who involves students in all phases of rule development, who facilitates active learning, and who monitors student behavior proactively by using a repertoire of management skills.

Although cooperative learning is an effective teaching strategy that motivates students to learn and reduces overall discipline problems, it is not a panacea for classroom management. The same types of discipline problems that have plagued teachers for generations will still exist. In fact, some behavior problems can become more critical when students start cooperative learning. Worse, the poor attitude of one student can destroy an entire group. If there are as many as five or six seriously disruptive students in a class, those students can make five or six groups dysfunctional, thus torpedoing effective group work. This problem becomes acute when teachers inherit an upper-grade class of disruptive students who have been "tracked" into low-level classes for years and who pride themselves on their "reputation." This book, therefore, will attempt to offer suggestions to manage the cooperative classroom by handling individual or class behavior problems so that teachers can respect their students' dignity, can maintain their own pride and control, and can build a caring and interactive atmosphere.

What Happened to that Old-Fashioned Discipline?

Fifty years ago, the topic of classroom control was virtually ignored in teacher education programs. Prospective teachers in those days were merely told to make good lesson plans, to be firm but gentle, and not to smile until Christmas. (McDaniel, 1986, p. 63)

The old-fashioned idea of "don't smile until Christmas" does not work. Unfortunately, many beginning teachers are more worried about "surviving" until Christmas rather than "smiling" by Christmas. According to Veenman, the Gallup polls of the '70s and '80s reported that the public believes that the answer to many of the problems that plague the schools is improved discipline. According to these same polls, teachers rated classroom management and discipline as their number-one concern (cited in Evertson & Harris, 1992). Faced with increasing numbers of special education students, bilingual students, "crack babies," economically disadvantaged youth, and children from broken families, teachers must now address myriad sociological, psychological, and educational problems that were non-existent when many veteran teachers took their educational methods courses in college. Glasser (1986) states, "Prior to WWII, we didn't have specific discipline programs. We maintained order in schools by throwing out the unruly and flunking out the unmotivated. Now we keep those students in school and try to find ways to keep them quiet" (p. 55).

Teachers today are often not prepared academically or emotionally to face these new challenges. They do not receive the staff development necessary to help them adapt to the new circumstances nor to adjust their teaching styles to meet the needs of the many new students who require a great deal more of their time and assistance.

Inclusion or Mainstreaming of Special Education Students

The Regular Education Initiative (REI) calls for the reform or radical reconstruction of special and general education. There are many components of this plan that are open to interpretation. One of the reforms REI calls for is changing eligibility requirements for special education. The first argument for such a change is that many students now served by special education could be taught in regular education classes. The second argument is that most or all students now identified as mildly or moderately handicapped would best be served by full-time placement in regular classrooms instead of being pulled out for services in separate settings (Executive Committe of the Council for Children with Behavioral Disorders, 1989). In British Columbia, the official position is that even the most severely handicapped child can benefit by inclusion or integration into the mainstream. Teachers there are encouraged to use a wide range of teaching methods, slow or accelerate the pace of instruction, use special materials, draw on support services, and, in some cases, identify additional learning outcomes for special needs students (Educational Programs Department, 1989, p. 10). Because of budget cuts and time constraints, many regular education teachers are now teaching these special education students through the inclusion or mainstreaming movement. However, these teachers have not had the staff development training to deal with these students' special needs, nor do they have the teacher's aides to accommodate the extra time and attention these students require. Therefore, teachers will need to learn how to foster positive interaction among all students and to monitor the learning and behavior of students with special needs. (Strategies will be discussed in Section 5.)

Increase in Bilingual Students

America has truly become a "salad bowl" as the twenty-first century approaches and school systems reflect the country's multicultural society. Between 1980 and 1990, the Hispanic population in the United States increased by forty-four percent. Asian and other populations increased by sixty-five percent (Hodgkinson, 1991, p. 12). Budget cuts have forced many school districts to reduce the number of bilingual teachers and teacher's aides; moreover, it is extremely expensive to provide services for students of all languages and dialects. Often, the classroom teacher will have as many as half of the class made up of non-English-speaking students. Classroom management problems, therefore, can become more severe because of communication problems.

The Changing Family

The American family continues to undergo changes. The "typical" family consisting of a married couple with children has declined in number while every kind of "atypical" family has increased. According to Hodgkinson (1991), 4.3 million children are living with a mother who has never married (up 678% since 1970). Today in America, one out of every four babies is born to an unmarried mother (Chapman, 1991). Because of the increase in the number of unmarried women having children and the high divorce rate, fifteen million children are being raised by single mothers who will have about one-third as much to spend on their needs as children being raised by two parents (Hodgkinson, 1991). Eitzen (1992) says that "children from single-parent families are less likely to be high achievers; they are consistently more likely to be late, truant, and subject to disciplinary action; and they are more than twice as likely to drop out of school" (p. 588).

Socio-Economic Issues

Economist Sylvia Ann Hewlett feels that America is facing profound and systematic child neglect. She says that more than twenty percent of all children are growing up in poverty. One of every five children under the age of eighteen could be classified as poor because his or her family's income for a family of three is below the $9,890 official poverty line. She also states that 330,000 children are homeless and twelve million children have little or no access to health care because they are uninsured (cited in Sullivan, 1991). If nothing is done to help them within the first five years, serious learning and behavior problems will doom these children to failure in school and possibly in life. Eitzen (1992) says the "downward social mobility" of today's society lowers the individual self-esteem and family honor of the "have nots." Some families cannot cope with adverse economic conditions and the family members experience stress, marital separation, divorce, depression, alcoholic tendencies, and spouse and child abuse. Children from such families often resort to "acting out," rejecting authority, running away, or experimenting with gangs, drugs, or sex to escape their situations or get attention. Again, regular and special education teachers must learn how to deal with the erratic behavior and the reduced academic abilities of these students and to recognize that traditional behavior programs and discipline models may not be effective.

Violence

School violence at one time seemed reserved for only inner city high schools. Today, however, gang violence, robberies, and shootings make headlines in elementary schools and in posh suburbs. The Federal Centers for Disease Control (as cited in Page, 1992) found that one student in five carries a weapon of some sort and one in twenty carries a gun. A fourth of the nation's school systems use metal detectors. Despite metal detectors, police guards, and six-foot fences around many schools, the number of young people killed by guns more than doubled from 1,059 in 1970 to 2,162 in 1990. Drive-by shootings, "drop drills" designed to teach students how to hit the ground when they hear gunfire, and gun fights during school dances and athletic contests occur with increasing regularity throughout this country (Page, 1992).

Besides the tremendous increase in violence against other students, the dramatic increase in violence against self is an indication of the feeling of helplessness and isolation felt by many young people. The suicide rate for teens aged fifteen to nineteen tripled between 1960 and 1986. Currently, 10.2 deaths out of every 100,000 are labeled suicides (Sullivan, 1991). Can the schools do more to help students cope with the pressures and problems of modern living?

Results of Problems

Many students must learn how to cope with dysfunctional families, drug and alcohol abuse, physical and sexual abuse, peer pressure, and a host of other problems. Memorizing chemical formulas or filling in ditto worksheets may not be the "satisfying" experiences and the lifelong learning skills these students need to function in the real world.

What happens when students are faced with all the pressures of modern life? Many students look to their school and their teachers to help them learn how to deal with their problems and gain the self-confidence and self-esteem they need to function in a social setting.

According to Glasser, however, many schools do not provide these "satisfying" and "relevant" experiences. Therefore, many students make the decision not to waste their time in a place that doesn't meet their needs. Many students choose to drop out of school. In fact, every eight seconds of the school day, one student drops out. According to the U.S. Department of Education, ten states had high school dropout rates over thirty percent. Florida led the list with 41.4 percent followed by Louisiana, 39.9; Michigan, 37.6; Georgia, 37.5; New York, 37.1; and Arizona, 35.6. Mississippi, Texas, California, Alaska, South Carolina, and Kentucky also record official dropout rates of over thirty percent (cited in Hodgkinson, 1991, p. 15).

Nationally, more than one-fourth of teenagers drop out of school. According to one study, these high school dropouts cost the nation more than $240 billion a year in lost earnings and forgone taxes (Sullivan, 1991, p. 5). Gage (1990) says that dropping out means less earning power. In 1986 male workers over age twenty-five who had completed four years of high school had a median annual income of $24,701; those with only some high school earned $20,000, or twenty percent less. This figure, however, doesn't take into consideration how many billions of dollars are spent by the government to cover the cost of social services, welfare, court costs, and prison costs that some of these dropouts eventually need. The Commission on Education in British Columbia is also concerned about "the disturbingly high dropout rate," and concludes that it needs to create relevant alternative programs of good quality to attract non-academic students who might otherwise leave school early (Educational Programs Department, 1989, p. 2).

Teacher Training

Few educational methods courses can prepare teachers for every problem they will encounter in the classroom. Moreover, many of the professors in colleges of education are neither exposed to nor trained in the types of methods courses needed by educators to help them cope with the wide assortment of academic and behavior problems they will most likely encounter. The California State

Legislature, however, took some steps in the 1980s to re-train professors who teach methods courses. The education reform bill requires the professors to return to the elementary or secondary classroom once every three years to get a truer picture of how students and education have changed (Warshaw, 1986). Regardless of improvements in college educational courses, however, the realities of the public school system in America are taking their toll on thousands of beginning and veteran teachers.

What Do the Experts Say?

Students need to feel that what they are studying is relevant, that they themselves are important, and that they can succeed. Glasser's assertion that "school must be meaningful and satisfying to the student" is important because only a discipline program that is also concerned with student satisfaction will work (Glasser, 1986, p. 56). Students should be able to say to themselves, "This school makes sense to me. I won't break the rules of a place in which I can get what I need" (Glasser as cited in Gough, 1987, p. 658).

Glasser warns against depending on a discipline program that is based on the stimulus/response psychology of doing something to students such as punishing them, writing their names on the board, or scaring or threatening them. These stimuli might work for the fifty percent of students who find school satisfying and who just need to be reminded of their responsibility every once in a while. These stimuli, however, will not work for the other fifty percent whose needs are not being met. Those students will continue to "act out" to get attention, power, revenge, or whatever else they need to feel satisfied. Punitive discipline tactics will not "bring them around." Glasser comments, "Our jails are filled with people who have been disciplined up to their ears—and, because most of them are lonely and powerless, they continue to commit crimes" (cited in Gough, 1987, p. 658).

Curwin and Mendler (1988) advocate informing students of the standards of acceptable behavior before those standards are violated and making sure that students know the specific rules and consequences. They also recommend that teachers and administrators stop misbehavior when it occurs without attacking the dignity of the student.

According to Curwin and Mendler, the goal in classroom management is to move from the "Obedience Model" where students behave when the teacher is present out of fear of being punished to the "Responsibility Model" where students behave because they have internalized appropriate behavior and they know it is the right thing to do.

McDaniel (1986) suggests that teachers could avoid many discipline problems by a few simple management techniques. If teachers use low-profile intervention to manage problems discreetly, unobtrusively, and smoothly, fewer disruptions will escalate to large-scale altercations that demand confrontation and action. "Teachers who are courteous, prompt, well-organized, enthusiastic, self-controlled, and patient tend to produce students who exhibit similar characteristics, at least to some degree" (McDaniel, 1986, p. 64).

The teacher sets the climate for the classroom. A teacher who cares about students will try to create a nurturing atmosphere in the class. Some of the ways to establish an atmosphere conducive to learning include the following:

1. Establishing a signal to get students' attention before starting to talk.
2. Appealing to different learning modalities by giving the instructions in both a verbal and written form.
3. Clearly stating the directions, requirements, and time limits.
4. Reviewing the methods of evaluation.
5. Monitoring the students' work and behavior.
6. Modeling the type of behavior and attitude expected of the students.
7. Addressing specific discipline problems in a confidential and discreet way.
8. Offering students some choice in assignments or methods of completing work.
9. Giving specific feedback and encouragement.
10. Maintaining a soft voice and cool head throughout a discipline altercation.

McDaniel (1986) argues that the quality of a teacher's discipline program ultimately rests on the quality of his or her instructional practices, ability to get along with children, and ability to convince young people that school is important. "School becomes important to children when teachers reach them with meaningful lessons and a professional attitude that says, I care about you; I know that you can behave; I want to help you to be a better you" (p. 67).

The method of discipline the teacher chooses will determine the atmosphere of the entire classroom. It should be noted, however, that effective classroom discipline is a means to achieve the desired result—enhanced student learning. Evertson and Harris (1992) found that educational research has expanded the definition of classroom management; moreover, research today is moving away from "a focus on controlling students' behavior and looks instead at teacher actions to create, implement, and maintain a classroom environment that supports learning" (p. 74). The most effective classroom management techniques in the world will not work unless those techniques are used in conjunction with meaningful content, active learning, and high expectations.

Kounin and Gump (cited in Everston & Harris, 1992, p. 75) identify strategies that teachers use to elicit high levels of work involvement and low levels of misbehavior:

- Withitness—communicating awareness of student behavior;
- Overlapping—doing more than one thing at once;
- Smoothness and Momentum—moving in and out of activities smoothly with appropriately paced and sequenced instruction; and
- Group alerting—keeping all students attentive in a whole-group focus.

The essential component of effective classroom management is that it "preserves" the time needed for meaningful instruction. Rather than wasting precious minutes starting class, passing back papers, getting into cooperative groups, and reprimanding errant students, teachers can teach. Walberg states that "the association of learning with time is among the most consistent that education research reveals" (cited in Evertson & Harris, 1992, p. 74).

Evertson and Harris (1992) reviewed past research and field studies on effective classroom management and found that teachers who are effective managers:

- use time as effectively as possible
- implement group strategies with high levels of involvement and low levels of misbehavior
- choose lesson formats and academic tasks conducive to high student engagement
- communicate clearly rules of participation
- prevent problems by implementing a system at the beginning of the school year (p. 76)

Time management, a system of procedures and rules developed early in the year, challenging and motivating academic tasks, and high-involvement group activities are essential components for creating and maintaining a classroom climate that promotes all aspects of learning.

The teacher must establish a warm and caring classroom climate and then work with the students to set the conditions under which they can develop their own sense of responsibility. The cooperative classroom fosters individual responsibility by allowing students to have choices, solve problems, make decisions, and be accountable for their work and their behavior. The days of the strict school teacher carrying the big stick are over. Students' behavior must be motivated by a sense of their own pride rather than a fear of punishment. Students should be allowed to participate in the formation of classroom rules, and they should be expected to conform to those rules. If the classroom climate is conducive to personal growth and development, students will be more likely to take responsibility for their actions—regardless of the circumstances of their lives outside school.

Review of Key Points of Research

Researchers	*Key Points*
Dreikurs	• All students want to belong.
	• All students want recognition.
	• Students who cannot get recognition in positive ways often misbehave.
	• Misbehavior is associated with four mistaken goals: attention getting, power seeking, revenge seeking, and displaying inadequacy.
	• Discipline is not punishment. It is teaching students how to be responsible for their own behavior.
	• Teachers should allow students to have a say in establishing classroom rules and consequences.
	• Teachers should teach students that consequences will always follow inappropriate behavior.
	• Teachers should encourage students to succeed, but not praise them or their actions.

Glasser

- All behavior is people's best attempt to control themselves to meet their needs.
- People always choose to do what is the most satisfying to them at the time.
- All people need to belong, to gain power, to be free, and to have fun.
- People feel pleasure when their needs are met and frustration when they are not.
- School must be meaningful to students.
- School must make sense to students.
- Teachers should not rely on stimulus/response psychology of punishing students to make them behave.
- Fifty percent of students are not getting their needs met in school.
- Students will "act out" to get attention, power, revenge, or anything else to feel satisfied if their needs aren't being met.
- Punitive measures will not "bring students around." (The jails are filled with persons who have been disciplined "up to their ears.")
- If schools are to have good disicpline, classes must contain fewer frustrated students and teachers.

Curwin & Mendler

Teachers should:
- Inform students of standards of acceptable behavior immediately.
- Make sure the students know the specific rules and consequences.
- Always respect the dignity of the students.
- Always handle discipline problems privately.
- Use the responsibility model where students behave because they know they should, not because they fear punishment.

McDaniel

Teachers should:

- Use low-profile interventions.
- Manage discipline problems discreetly.
- Be courteous, well-organized, prompt, enthusiastic, self-controlled, and patient (and students will model those characteristics).
- Set the climate for the classroom.
- Appeal to students' learning styles.
- Give clear directions—both verbal and written.
- Offer students some choice in assignments.
- Maintain a soft voice and a cool head throughout disciplinary situations.

Kounin & Gump

Teachers should:

- Achieve "withitness" by communicating awareness of student behavior.
- Effectively "overlap" or do more than one thing at once.
- Demonstrate "smoothness and momentum" in moving in and out of activities.
- Avoid "slow downs"—delays that waste time between activities.
- Keep all students attentive in a whole-group focus.

Evertson & Harris

Teachers should:

- Use time effectively.
- Implement group strategies with high levels of involvement and low levels of misbehavior.
- Choose lesson formats and academic tasks conducive to high student engagement.
- Clearly communicate rules of participation.
- Prevent problems by implementing a system at the beginning of the school year.

Johnson & Johnson	• Children do not instinctively know how to cooperate with others.
	• Many elementary and secondary students lack basic social skills.
	• Students who lack appropriate social skills find themselves isolated, alienated, and disadvantaged in school and careers.
	• Poor peer relationships have long-term effects on students' cognitive and social development, well-being, happiness, and psychological health.
	• A cooperative context must be established in the classroom.
	• Cooperative skills have to be directly taught.
	• Group members determine whether the social skills are learned and internalized.
	• Students should be taught cooperative skills at an early age.
Bellanca & Fogarty	• Most students respond to the informal social skills woven into the classroom expectations, roles, and guidelines.
	• Many students, however, require more formal direction in acquiring the cooperative social skills.
	• Students need to be taught how to form groups, how to interact in groups, and how to handle conflicts.
	• Social skills can be taught in four stages:
	- the Hook lesson lays the groundwork
	- the T-Chart or web helps students generate specific behaviors
	- guided practice helps students reinforce and internalize the skills
	- observation of the targeted skill gives the students feedback to refine the skill
Kohn	• Moral concerns and social skills should be taught in schools.

- Competition and self-interest are counter-productive.
- Teachers should use a well-designed program of prosocial instruction that includes cooperative conflict resolution.
- The development of prosocial values (especially in a cooperative learning classroom) enhances academic achievement.
- Punishment is not an effective discipline technique.
- Bribing students with rewards and incentives is an artificial attempt to manipulate behavior.
- Students should become responsible for their behavior by internalizing good behavior.
- The value of the group or community should be internalized in students.
- Students need to be part of the decision-making process of classroom procedures, learning, goals, and problem solving.

This book will attempt to synthesize the research on classroom discipline, management techniques, and cooperative learning. This synthesis will help teachers develop a classroom atmosphere that allows students to develop responsible behaviors within the parameters of high teacher expectations and an organizational framework.

ORGANIZATION OF THIS BOOK

This book will address discipline problems at four levels.

1. **Cooperative Group Problems**—Some cooperative groups will not function because of personality or organizational problems. A dysfunctional group can undermine the cooperative classroom.

2. **Individual Behavior Problems**—Often a few students can "torpedo" a group or class because of their inappropriate behavior. Individual behavior problems need to be handled quickly, quietly, and appropriately.

3. **Students with Special Needs**—Students with language challenges, physical handicaps, or learning disabilities often need special help to meet their academic and social needs.

4. **Whole Class**—Teachers need to use appropriate methods to deal with discipline problems that disrupt the entire class and impede learning for everyone.

In Part I, chapters one, two, and three discuss establishing procedures, rules, consequences, and a positive classroom climate. Chapters four, five, six, and seven deal with forming cooperative groups and teaching the social skills of basic interaction, communicating within groups, building team skills, and resolving conflicts.

Part II of this book deals with "The Challenges." Strategies are introduced to help students who have trouble with responsibility, students with weak interpersonal skills, students with serious behavior problems, and students with special needs.

Each chapter begins with a short scenario of a problem situation. Possible solutions to the problem are suggested, and then individuals or groups are asked to brainstorm their own solutions and sequence the steps they feel will help solve the problem.

At the end of each brainstorming section, individuals are asked to reflect on similar discipline problems they have encountered and write how they might handle the problem in the future.

The Epilogue, "When All the Kids Misbehave," deals with strategies to try when the entire class gets off track and needs a refresher lesson on social skills. The class meeting scenario addresses the issues in a democratic forum and proposes solutions to which both the teacher and the students can agree.

Part

I

The Rules of the Game

DISCIPLINE IN THE CLASSROOM

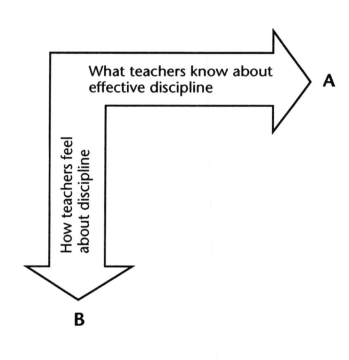

What teachers know about effective discipline

How teachers feel about discipline

A
- *Limit the number of classroom rules to five*
- *Students should have input into rules*
- *Rules can change throughout the year*
- *Some rules are non-negotiable*
- *Consequences should be logical*
- *Class rules should be consistent with school rules*

B

- *I don't always agree with the school rules*
- *Sometimes rules are unenforceable*
- *I am not always consistent enforcing the rules*
- *I sometimes have to make exceptions to the rules*
- *I get angry when other teachers don't enforce school rules*

Discipline in the Classroom

The more students are involved in the process of developing rules and consequences, the more they feel that the plan is a part of them. Ultimately, they will follow the plan if they had a say in its development. (Curwin & Mendler, 1988, p. 52)

The idea of including students in the process of developing classroom rules and consequences is still considered "radical" by many educators. Traditionally, teachers spent days composing a list of rules and then ritualistically presented them to students as they walked into class the first day of school. It is still not unusual for teachers to prepare four pages of rules that cover everything from gum chewing to knuckle cracking. And, of course, punishments for breaking these rules are listed in equally great detail. Almost everyone can remember an unusual or Draconian punishment suffered at the hands of a teacher. Punishments that include sitting in the garbage can all day, pushing an eraser around the room with one's nose, standing in the corner, making a public apology, being shut in a closet, or walking around with gum on the nose all day may seem humorous and archaic, but the effects they have on students is not funny; they leave their mark on the students for life.

Curwin and Mendler refer to the system of strict rules and punishments as the Obedience Model. According to this model, students will follow the rules because they are told to, regardless of their own ideas of right and wrong. Curwin and Mendler (1988) state, "In the short term, obedience offers teachers relief, a sense of power and control, and an oasis from the constant bombardment of defiance. In the long run, however, obedience leads to student immaturity, a lack of responsibility, an inability to think clearly and critically, and a feeling of helplessness that is manifested by withdrawal, aggressiveness, or power struggles" (p. 23).

In the Obedience Model, students fear punishment for breaking a rule. Kohn (1991) feels that punishment teaches nothing about what a student is supposed to do—only about what he is *not* supposed to do. Therefore, rather than develop responsibility and an internal locus of control, students instead focus all their energies on how to get away with misbehavior. Not getting caught supersedes everything else in the game of teacher versus student. The strict obedience model of management is not working. Teachers need to collaborate with students to create a caring and cooperative classroom where eveyone contributes, everyone is responsible for his her own behavior, and everyone is concerned about each other.

1

Getting Started

"**I** *feel it is very important that we always walk in the halls and enter the room slowly. Why do you think that procedure is important?*" asks Mrs. Saunders.

"*I saw a boy get hurt once when another boy was rushing into the room and knocked him into the doorknob real hard,*" Mary replies.

"*I don't like getting shoved by someone who is afraid of being late,*" adds John.

"*So, you think we should all be courteous and enter the room walking rather than running or shoving?*" Mrs. Saunders asks.

"*Yes,*" says the class.

"*All right, let's practice how we should all enter the room. Everyone file out quietly and stand by the drinking fountain down the hall. When I give the signal, you will all walk toward our classroom and enter the room the way we discussed.*"

Students rehearse entering the classroom and taking their seat.

"*I really liked the way you took turns entering the room and going to your desks. Now,*

*what do you think would be a consequence if someone forgot our procedure and ran
into someone while running into the room?"*

*"I think that person should have to go back and practice walking into the room
again just like we practiced today,"* says Juan.

*"He should also have to apologize to whoever he ran into 'cause no one likes to be
pushed,"* Jack adds.

"Okay," says Mrs. Saunders, *"I think we all agree on the importance of this
procedure. We'll add this to our list of classroom procedures and consequences."*

THE NEED FOR STRUCTURE

Very few students function well in a chaotic environment. Even
though students may pretend to like the freedom to do whatever
they want, whenever they want, most of them prefer structures or
routines so they know exactly what they are supposed to do.

Teachers can be creative and structure open-ended cooperative
activities that allow students lots of options and choices. However,
students need to "walk" before they can "run," and it is essential
that they know their boundaries the first week of class. Teachers
should prepare a tentative list of procedures they feel are necessary for establishing routines that are essential for the organization of the classroom; however, the entire class should discuss the
rationale for the procedures and have some input in their final
adoption.

The most effective way to handle discipline problems is to
prevent them. The proactive teacher anticipates potential management problems and establishes a positive classroom environment where students feel secure because they know what is
expected of them.

Researchers in the area of classroom management offer the
following tips for teachers:

1. Proactive teachers help prevent discipline problems.
2. Students who are actively involved in the lessons cause
   fewer behavior problems.
3. Teachers who use instructional time efficiently have fewer
   management problems.

Good classroom management is primarily *prevention,* not intervention, *planning* before the year begins, *implementing* on the first
day of school, and *maintaining* consistently throughout the year.

"Procedures are ways of getting class activities done. Their function is to routinize tasks for continuity, predictability, and time saving" (Evertson and Harris, 1991b, p. 2). They recommend four steps in teaching classroom procedures:

1. Explain
    a. give concrete definition of procedures
    b. provide the reason or rationale
    c. demonstrate the procedure
    d. present the task step by step
    e. explain and demonstrate cues
2. Rehearse the procedure.
3. Provide feedback to individuals and the class.
4. Re-teach procedures as necessary. (Evertson and Harris, 1991b, p. 2)

The procedures in a class should relate to the important principles that permeate the classroom climate. If students are expected to be prepared, on time, courteous, and respectful of others' rights, the procedures should support those principles. Courteous and responsible behavior builds cooperation and team work. Students feel obliged to treat other students the way they would like to be treated.

Teachers need to decide on the types of procedures that will be needed for their students and be prepared to discuss the procedures during the first few days of school. Some procedures may be *negotiable,* and some procedures will be *non-negotiable.* Some of the procedures may have consequences if they are violated (see Chapter 2 for a discussion of the difference between "punishment" and "consequence"). The teacher and the students should discuss the necessity of the procedures offered by the teacher, vote on their adoption, and post them in the room.

Many of the procedures should be rehearsed or role-played, and the teacher should gently remind students of the procedures by standing close to the student and pointing to the list of procedures posted in the room.

The key to effective procedures is consistency. If a procedure isn't working, discuss it and change it. But if the procedure is necessary and it is on the list, enforce it. The breakdown in classroom management doesn't usually start with a bang—it starts with a whimper!

Assignment #1

CLASSROOM PROCEDURES: DO STUDENTS KNOW WHAT IS EXPECTED OF THEM FOR ROUTINE OPERATIONS?

Prepare a list of procedures you think are necessary to perform routine operations to present to the students for discussion. The procedures will vary depending on the age level of the students. Check the categories that apply to your situation. Then use the blank form to create your own final list.

A. Beginning the Class

- ❑ How should students enter the room?
- ❑ What constitutes being late (in the room, in the seat)?
- ❑ How and when will absentee slips will be handled?
- ❑ What type of seating arrangements will be used (assigned seats, open seating, cooperative group seating)?
- ❑ How will students get materials (materials manager in group, first student in each row, designated person)?
- ❑ How will the teacher get students' attention to start class (the tardy bell, raised hand, lights turned off and on)?

B. Classroom Management

- ❑ How and when will students leave their seats?
- ❑ What do students need in order to leave the room (individual passes, room pass, teacher's permission)?
- ❑ How will students get help from teacher (raise hands, put name on board, ask other group members first)?
- ❑ What are acceptable noise levels for discussion, group work, seat work?
- ❑ How should students work with other students (moving desks, changing seats, noise level, handling materials)?
- ❑ How will students get recognized to talk (raised hand, teacher calls on student, talk out)?

C. Paper Work

- ❑ How will students turn in work (put in specific tray or box, pass to the front, one student collects)?
- ❑ How will students turn in make-up work if they were absent (special tray, give to teacher, put in folder, give to teacher's aide)?
- ❑ How will students distribute handouts (first person in row, a group member gets a copy for all group members, students pick up as they enter room)?
- ❑ How will late work be graded (no penalty, minus points, zero, "F," use lunch or recess to finish, turn in by end of day, drop so many homework grades)?

© 1992 Skylight Publishing

❑ How and when will students make up quizzes and tests missed (same day they return to school, within twenty-four hours, within the week, before school, during lunch or recess, after school)?

❑ How will late projects such as research papers, portfolios, and art work will be graded (no penalty, minus points, lowered letter grade, no late work accepted)?

D. Dismissal from Class or School

❑ When do students leave class for the day (when bell rings, when teacher gives the signal)?

❑ Can students stay after class to finish assignments, projects, tests?

❑ Can the teacher keep one student or the whole class after class or school?

E. Syllabus or Course Outline

❑ How are students made aware of course objectives?

❑ How are students made aware of course requirements?

❑ Are students given due dates for major assignments several weeks in advance?

❑ Are students told how they will be evaluated and given the grading scale?

F. Other Procedures

(You may need to introduce procedures related to recess, assemblies, guest speakers, substitute teachers, field trips, fire drills, teacher leaving the room, etc.)

BLANK PROCEDURES FORM

Grade Level _____   Subject Area _____

A. Beginning the Class

❑ _____

❑ _____

❑ _____

❑ _____

❑ _____

B. Classroom Management

❑ _____

❑ _____

❑ _____

❑ _____

❑ _____

C. Paper Work

❑ _____
❑ _____
❑ _____
❑ _____
❑ _____

D. Dismissal from Class or School

❑ _____
❑ _____
❑ _____
❑ _____
❑ _____

E. Syllabus or Course Outline

❑ _____
❑ _____
❑ _____
❑ _____
❑ _____

F. Bringing Books, Notebooks, and Supplies to Class

❑ _____
❑ _____
❑ _____
❑ _____
❑ _____

G. Other Procedures

❑ _____
❑ _____
❑ _____
❑ _____
❑ _____

Assignment #2

Brainstorm possible procedures that you think will need to be discussed with your students.

© 1992 Skylight Publishing

Who Makes the Rules?

"**O***kay class,*" begins Mrs. Baker. "*I see that one of the rules on our web is 'Students should raise their hands to speak!' Let's talk about that rule before we vote on it.*"

"*I don't like that rule,*" Mary offers. "*When I get an idea, I have to blurt it out quickly or I'll lose it.*"

"*Yeah,*" Sam agrees. "*I hate holding my hand up waiting for the teacher to call on me. It's a hassle.*"

"*All right, Mary and Sam have some legitimate concerns about the rule. Let's role play a situation and see if we can get a handle on this problem. I'll start talking about the Middle Ages, and we'll allow students to talk without raising their hands.*"

"*One of the major problems confronting the people in the Middle Ages was the Bubonic Plague. Researchers estimate that as many as one-third the population of Europe died because of the plague. One interesting thing about...*"

"*Is that like AIDS today?*" Jimmy interrupts.

"*Didn't rats spread the plague?*" wonders Susan.

"Oh yuk, I hate rats!" shouts Juanita.

"Ooh, I saw a movie about these rats that take over a whole city. It was gross!" Sam adds.

"Well, my sister has a pet rat and he's not gross." Susan retorts.

"Are you kidding? My next door neighbor has a pet snake. I bet it eats rats!" yells Jimmy.

Finally, Mrs. Baker says, *"Umm, let's see. Yes, Jimmy, we are going to talk later about how the plague compares to AIDS, and yes, Susan, the plague was spread by the fleas on rats. We'll be talking about that more tomorrow. Let's see, what else?"*

"Stop!" yells Mary. *"I think I understand why we need to raise our hands to speak. When people blurt things out, we get off track. Also, it's rude to interrupt our teacher in the middle of her sentence."*

"I'm glad you can see how easy it is to get off track when somebody talks in the middle of my idea," says Mrs. Baker.

"I agree," Sam says. *"I don't like people interrupting me. I can see how you can finish your idea and then call on someone. I'll vote for it!"*

"Let's take a vote. All those in favor of passing the rule to raise our hands to get recognized before we speak, please raise your hand!" says Mrs. Baker.

"Great, 32 in favor; 3 opposed. By virtue of this class meeting, we hereby pass Rule #1. Elsa, please write it on our list on the wall."

CLASSROOM RULES

If classroom procedures form the framework for a classroom climate conducive to students and teachers working together cooperatively, the classroom rules form the heart and soul of caring, cooperative classrooms. If students are going to "buy into" the system, they must be a part of the process.

According to Kohn (1991), "an immense body of research has shown that children are more likely to follow a rule if its rationale has been explained to them . . . . Discipline based on reason is more effective than the totalitarian approach captured by the T-shirt slogan 'Because I'm the Mommy, that's why'" (Kohn, 1991, p. 502).

Curwin and Mendler (1988) feel that effective rules describe specific behavior. They also believe that effective rules should be built on principles like honesty, courtesy, helpfulness, and the like. Evertson and Harris (1991b, p. 2) offer eight guidelines for writing classroom rules.

Rules should be . . .

1. Consistent with school rules
2. Understandable
3. Doable (students able to comply)
4. Manageable
5. Always applicable (consistent)
6. Stated positively
7. Stated behaviorally
8. Consistent with teacher's own philosophy of how students learn best

Clearly stated rules that describe specific behavior enable students to understand what is expected of them. If rules are too specific, however, too many rules will be needed. For example:

Too general: "Students shouldn't bother other students."

Too specific: "Students should not grab, push, shove, or trip other students."

Better rule: "It is best that students keep their hands off other people."

It is imperative that students get an opportunity to discuss the proposed classroom rules and understand the rationale behind the rules. A class meeting is the perfect opportunity to have a frank discussion of the rules, role-play situations, and come to a class consensus about the rules the students and teacher will adopt in order to ensure a positive and organized classroom environment. (For further discussion of an all-class meeting, see the Epilogue.)

It is important to note here that some rules are non-negotiable. Students must understand that the school district or the school sets down some rules that are not subject to a vote. Rules related to fighting, damage to property, injury to self or others are absolute; therefore, they set parameters for all students in order to ensure their health and safety.

After the class members and teacher have come to consensus on their classroom rules, they should discuss and agree on the logical consequences students will face if they violate the rules. The old-fashioned "punishment" paradigm is not effective. As Kohn (1991) states, "reliance on the threat of punishment is a reasonably good indication that something is wrong in a classroom, since children have to be bullied into acting the way the teacher demands" (p. 500).

If teachers are to establish an atmosphere of cooperation where students assume responsibility for their actions, the old obedience model of "spare the rod, spoil the child" is ineffectual. Kohn (1991) notes that "isolating a child from his peers, humiliating her, giving him an F, loading her with extra homework, or even threatening to do any of these things can produce compliance in the short run. Over the long run, however, this strategy is unproductive" (p. 500).

Consequences, on the other hand, relate directly to the rule violation and seem more logical and just than punishments. Curwin and Mendler (1988) warn, however, that "a consequence can become a punishment if it is delivered aggressively" (p. 65). According to Curwin and Mendler (1988, p. 66-69) consequences work best when they:

1. are clear and specific
2. have a range of alternatives
   a. reminder
   b. warning [or second reminder]
   c. conference with student
   d. conference with parent and/or administrator
3. are not punishments
4. are natural and/or logical
5. are related to the rule

For example, if a student violates the rule about homework by not completing it, the consequence would not logically be to send that student to the principal. The consequence would more logically involve having the student turn in the homework before the end of the day, stay in from recess or lunch to finish it, or lose points. Consequences relate directly to the rule violation. Across-the-board punishments such as "sit in the corner," "go to the office," or "miss the field trip" are punitive.

Punishment often diminishes the dignity of the student as well as breeds resentment and resistance. Kohn (1991) says that punishment teaches nothing about what a student is supposed to do—only about what he is not supposed to do. Curwin and Mendler (1988) feel that if students are only motivated by a reward-and-punishment system, they will only behave out of fear of getting caught rather than out of a sense of social responsibility. And Glasser (1990) warns that students will not be coerced into doing anything. They must see the rationale behind the rules and they must be a part of the process.

Some effective generic consequences might include the following:

First offense	Reminder
Second offense	Second Reminder
Third offense	Conference with student
Fourth offense	Social contract with student
Fifth offense	Conference with parent and administrators

Other consequences should be specifically related to the rule.

Examples

Rule
Students will be in their seats when the bell rings.

Consequences
1. Reminder
2. Second Reminder
3. Student must find out what he or she missed and make it up
4. Conference with student
5. Social contract
6. Conference with parent

Rule
Students will hand in homework on day it is due.

Consequences
1. Reminder
2. Second Reminder
3. Conference with student
4. Points subtracted from grade
5. Conference with parent

If students have some input in the establishment of the consequences, they are more likely to recognize fairness and logic in their implementation. Furthermore, students who accept their consequences, realizing they have not fulfilled their responsibility or obligation, are likely to learn from their mistakes.

Behavior Checklists

Hopefully, most students will accept the "rule and consequence" paradigm, internalize their own responsibilities, and model the positive behavior of their peers and teacher. The need will still exist, however, to chronicle the behavior of those who choose not to cooperate. It is imperative that the documentation of all violations remain private and confidential.

The teacher can use a grade book, checklists, or any type of written format to monitor disruptive behavior. Writing the names of misbehaving students on the blackboard and adding checks after their names for repeat offenses, however, is not conducive to establishing classroom trust, nor does it build the self-esteem of the students.

No teacher wants to take time away from teaching to be an "accountant" whose job is to debit and credit discipline violations, but there are ways to monitor student behavior efficiently. The following checklists may help keep track of violations without embarrassing students or losing instructional time. It is suggested that teachers record specific dates under each rule violation in order to determine which consequence would apply and to document persistent discipline problems in case more formal referrals are required later.

Classroom Rules and Consequences

Teacher: _____   Class: _____   Date: _____

Rule #1: _____

       Consequences 1. _____
                            2. _____
                            3. _____
                            4. _____
                            5. _____

Rule #2: _____

       Consequences 1. _____
                            2. _____
                            3. _____
                            4. _____
                            5. _____

Rule #3: _____

       Consequences 1. _____
                            2. _____
                            3. _____
                            4. _____
                            5. _____

Rule #4: _____

       Consequences 1. _____
                            2. _____
                            3. _____
                            4. _____
                            5. _____

Rule #5: _____

       Consequences 1. _____
                            2. _____
                            3. _____
                            4. _____
                            5. _____

© 1992 Skylight Publishing

Behavior Checklist

Teacher: _____   Class: _____   Date: _____

Write the date of each violation under the rule that the student violated.

Behavior Checklist

Names	Rule 1	Rule 2	Rule 3	Rule 4	Rule 5
1. John Doe	9/15, 10/3		11/1	12/6	
2.					
3.					
4.					
5.					
6.					
7.					
8.					
9.					
10.					
11.					
12.					
13.					
14.					
15.					
16.					
17.					
18.					
19.					
20.					
21.					
22.					
23.					
24.					
25.					
26.					
27.					
28.					
29.					
30.					

SKYLIGHT PUBLISHING, INC.

Discipline Checklist

Class: _____ Teacher: _____ Date:_____

Rules:	**Consequences:**

Rule #1 _____ 1. _____

Rule #2 _____ 2. _____

Rule #3 _____ 3. _____

Rule #4 _____ 4. _____

Rule #5 _____ 5. _____

Write the dates of all violations in boxes under rule numbers.

Class Roll	Rule					Comments
	1	2	3	4	5	
1.						
2.						
3.						
4.						
5.						
6.						
7.						
8.						
9.						
10.						
11.						
12.						
13.						
14.						
15.						
16.						
17.						
18.						
19.						
20.						

SKYLIGHT PUBLISHING, INC.

Assignment #1

Evertson and Harris (1991b, p. 2) establish some guidelines for effective rules:

1. Consistent with school rules
2. Understandable
3. Doable (students able to comply)
4. Always applicable
5. Consistent
6. Stated positively
7. Stated behaviorally
8. Consistent with teacher's own philosophy of how students learn best

Review the following rules and check if they fit the above criteria for classroom rules. If so, mark the rule "Yes." If not, mark it "No" and rewrite it to make it a "Yes."

Rules Students will:	**YES**	**NO**
1. Not talk out of turn. Rewrite:_____	❑	❑
2. Be considerate of others. Rewrite:_____	❑	❑
3. Not hit others. Rewrite:_____	❑	❑
4. Respect the property of others. Rewrite:_____	❑	❑
5. Not use profanity. Rewrite:_____	❑	❑

Assignment #2

Use the web graphic organizer to have students brainstorm the rules they feel are needed for their classroom. Assign groups of three to fill out a group web, and then complete a class web where all ideas are included.

Assignment #3

1. Select either elementary, middle school, or high school level.

    Circle one: elementary middle school high school

2. List common types of behavior problems in the category you selected.

Common behavior problems for students in _____ school.

A. _____
B. _____
C. _____
D. _____
E. _____
F. _____
G. _____

3. Generate a list of five rules and the logical consequences for those rules if students violate them for the level you selected.

*Rule #1:*_____

Logical Consequences:

   a._____
   b._____
   c._____
   d._____
   e._____
   f._____

*Rule #2:*_____

Logical Consequences:

   a._____
   b._____
   c._____
   d._____
   e._____
   f._____

*Rule #3:*_____

Logical Consequences:

   a._____
   b._____
   c._____
   d._____
   e._____
   f._____

*Rule #4:*_____

Logical Consequences:

a._____

b._____

c._____

d._____

e._____

f._____

*Rule #5:*_____

Logical Consequences:

a._____

b._____

c._____

d._____

e._____

f._____

4. Predict what rules could be eliminated as students internalize them and they become unnecessary.

Rules That Could Be Eliminated:

_____

_____

_____

_____

_____

_____

_____

_____

5. Predict what additional rules could be developed throughout the year as students master the basic social skills and begin developing skills in conflict resolution.

Additional Rules:

_____

_____

_____

_____

_____

_____

_____

_____

SKYLIGHT
PUBLISHING, INC.

3

Establishing a Cooperative, Responsible Classroom

"**I** hate doing these geometry problems," groans Chuck. *"Why will we need to know this for life? We spend half the class working these theorems!"*

"What's the problem, Chuck?" asks Mrs. Nordstrom.

"Math is boring," Chuck explodes.

"Now, Chuck," Mrs. Nordstrom replies. *"Things are not boring—people who don't understand them just think they're boring."*

"I understand the problems," shouts Chuck. *"I just don't give a d____!"*

"If you understand so much," says Mrs. Nordstrom through gritted teeth, her voice rising, *"Why did you have so much trouble on your last test?"*

"Because I wanted to flunk—it was my personal best."

Now angry, Mrs. Nordstrom says, *"All right, young man. You can just march yourself down to the principal's office right now."*

"Great, I'd rather sit in the office all day then sit in this stupid room!"

SETTING THE CLIMATE

The goal of all teachers is to provide powerful and stimulating lessons so that the students become so "hooked" on the lesson and the group interaction that they have no time to misbehave. The reality, of course, is that no matter how dynamic the teacher and the lesson are, there will always be the student who will try to torpedo any activity by making a "big splash" in the class, creating a whirlpool effect to "pull down" the other students. The teacher's job is to make sure that "big splash" only causes a ripple effect. A few students may succumb to the pull of the disruptive kid, but the rest will manage to "stay afloat" because of the teacher's ability to create his or her own whirlpool of interest, motivation, and respect.

The 80-15-5 Principle

Curwin and Mendler (1988) found that there are generally three groups of students in every classroom setting. About eighty percent of students rarely break the rules. They come to school to learn, and they have been fairly successful. Fifteen percent of the students break the rules on a somewhat regular basis, vary in their grades from high to low depending on the teacher or the class, and will disrupt learning for others if they don't have structure and a clear set of rules and consequences. The last five percent cause the most problems:

> These students are chronic rule breakers and are generally out of control most of the time. Nothing seems to work for them. They have typically experienced failure in school from an early age and maintain no hope for success in the future. They believe they have no reason to behave or to learn. Some have severe learning or emotional problems and may come from troubled homes. (Curwin & Mendler, 1988, p. 28)

The 80-15-5 principle presents a challenge for teachers. Those who teach basic skills or remedial courses or electives where counselors tend to schedule "problem students" so they'll have success or learn a trade may even have a fifty-fifty split of students motivated to learn and students motivated to disrupt. Needless to say, the teacher will have to spend some time preventing disruptive students from drowning the entire class.

Publicly embarrassing or humiliating students, however, will not make students learn from their mistakes; it will make them try harder not to get caught and it will often make them resentful. As Glasser (1986) states, "For thousands of years we have wrongly concluded that what we do *to* or *for* people can make them behave the way we want even if it does not satisfy them" (p. 20).

Dealing with disruptive students in private, in a fair and consistent manner, and in a manner that maintains their dignity and self-esteem will help them develop an "internal locus of control" and responsibility. Students with an internal locus of control feel guilty when they misbehave, learn from their mistakes, are able to accept the consequences for their actions, and know they can control their actions.

Dealing with disruptive students in front of their peers in an emotional outburst of frustration and anger, however, will lower their self-concept, decrease their desire to cooperate and succeed, and prevent them from developing their own sense of responsibility. They will learn how to become defensive and use an "external locus of control" to blame others for their problems. Consequently, these students rarely accept responsibility for their own actions. Public reprimands, moreover, will eventually destroy the positive climate in any classroom. Students will not feel free to engage in interactive discussions, contribute ideas, or share experiences if they are never sure when they will incur the teacher's wrath or become the object of the teacher's sarcasm or anger. Respecting the dignity of each and every student is essential for effective classroom management.

Teacher Behaviors that Can Erode the Classroom Climate

If students perceive that the teacher is treating them unfairly, they may label that teacher "unfair" or "the enemy." The seeds of insurrection may then be planted, making a small discipline incident escalate into a major discipline problem.

Teachers need to be careful in their enforcement of classroom rules and consequences. Sometimes the "message" can be fair, consistent, and positive, but the "delivery system" can be sarcastic, punitive, and negative. Teachers need to model a cooperative value system by treating their own students just like they want their students to treat one another. Some of the essential rules for effective group work can apply to teacher/student interactions.

The following "Dirty Dozen" describe the types of teacher behavior that can erode a positive classroom climate and undermine any discipline program—no matter how democratic. Teachers in both subtle and blatant ways can send signals to individual students and to the whole class that jeopardize the caring, cooperative classroom.

Burke's "Dirty Dozen"
Teacher Behaviors that Can Erode the Classroom Climate

1. **Sarcasm** Students' feelings can be hurt by sarcastic put-downs thinly disguised as "humor."

2. **Negative Tone of Voice** Students can "read between the lines" and sense a sarcastic, negative, or condescending tone of voice.

3. **Negative Body Language** Clenched fists, a set jaw, a quizzical look, or standing over a student in a threatening manner can speak more loudly than any words.

4. **Inconsistency** Nothing escapes the students' attention. They will be the first to realize the teacher is not enforcing the rules consistently.

5. **Favoritism** "Brown-nosing" is an art and any student in any class can point out the "teacher's pet" who gets special treatment. There are no secrets in a class!

6. **Put-Downs** Sometimes teachers are not aware they are embarrassing a student with subtle put-downs, but if teachers expect students to encourage rather than put down, they need to model positive behavior.

7. **Outbursts** Teachers are sometimes provoked by students and they "lose it." These teacher outbursts set a bad example for the students, create a negative climate, and could lead to more serious problems.

8. **Public Reprimands** No one wants to be corrected or humiliated in front of his peers. One way to make an enemy out of a student is to make him or her lose face in front of the other students.

9. **Unfairness** Taking away promised privileges or rewards; scheduling a surprise test; "nitpicking" while grading homework or tests; or assigning punitive homework could be construed by students as being "unfair."

10. **Apathy** Students want teachers to listen to them, show them they are important, and empathize with them. If teachers convey the attitude that teaching is just a job and students are just aggravations that must be dealt with, students will respond accordingly.

11. **Inflexibility** Some students may need extra help or special treatment in order to succeed. A teacher should be flexible enough to "bend the rules" or adjust the standards to meet students' individual needs.

12. **Lack of Humor** Teachers who cannot laugh at themselves usually have problems motivating students to learn, and usually have boring classes.

 SKYLIGHT PUBLISHING, INC.

The Last Resort: The Principal

Even if teachers provide quality lessons that stimulate students' ideas and relate to real-life situations, and even if they are proactive, there will always be that hard-core "five percent" group of students who will choose to disrupt the rest of the class because the class does not satisfy their needs or because their desire for attention, power, or recognition supersedes their need to learn.

It is the teacher's responsibility to make sure these disruptive students do not destroy the positive atmosphere of the class and cooperative spirit of the learning teams. If teachers do their best to anticipate potential behavior problems, diffuse minor problems before they become major disturbances, and address disruptive behaviors immediately, they should be able to counteract most problems. However, once the teacher has done everything possible to solve the problem and to control the student's negative behavior, he or she must resort to outside help—the administration. Sending a student to the principal is not a cop-out, unless, of course, it is done at the first sign of a problem.

Teachers should never relinquish their position of authority early on in an altercation with a student or they will lose the respect of that student, and possibly the whole class. The teacher is no longer in control; the administrator is. If, however, the teacher has exhausted his or her repertoire of strategies, the student's behavior has not improved, and the disruptive behavior is negatively influencing the entire class, the last resort becomes the next step. The student may also have to be referred to the school counselor, psychologist, special education coordinator, or social worker. Accurate documentation of the student's behavior (dates, incidents, actions taken) will be important.

Proactive Teachers

The effective classroom teacher anticipates the types of problems that could occur in the classroom and develops a repertoire of strategies to solve the problems. The type of *proactive* approach to preventing discipline problems *before* they occur is far less time-consuming than the *reactive* approach where teachers expend all their energy trying to solve problems *after* they occur. The following procedures could be utilized by the proactive teacher.

Proactive Approaches to Teaching

1. Anticipate Potential Behavior Problems
   - Don't allow potential problem students to sit together or work together in groups.
   - Seat problem students close to the teacher.
   - Give both verbal and written directions to eliminate confusion and frustration that often lead to behavior problems.
   - Structure assignments that are relevant, motivating, and developmentally appropriate.
   - Follow Glasser's second principle for Quality Schools (in Brantigan & McElliot, 1991) where students are only asked to do school work they agree has "quality." Don't coerce students into learning facts that, by themselves, have no use in the outside world. Don't teach or test for nonsense.
   - Allow enough time for students to complete assignments.
   - Make allowances for students with learning disabilities or physical handicaps so they are not frustrated and overwhelmed.
   - Pair the potential problem student with a helpful and nurturing partner.
   - Encourage peer tutoring to help weaker students complete their work without becoming frustrated.
   - Assign a potentially disruptive student to observe an effective cooperative group.
   - Conference with students prone to behavior problems to find out if they have some personal or family problems that might be causing them to be upset or uncooperative.
   - Talk with parents to find out about any medical problems the student might have.
   - Talk with counselors or support personnel to find out about any previous behavior problems the student might have experienced and get suggestions about how to best meet the individual needs of the students.

2. Diffuse Minor Problems Before They Become Major Disturbances

   Proximity
   - Move close to the student when you sense a problem developing.

Student-Selected Time Out

- Allow the student to select a time-out from the class or the group. Let the student go to a desk or chair in the corner of the room to "collect his thoughts" or calm down.

Teacher-Selected Time Out

- Ask the student to go to the time-out area to complete work when his or her behavior is disrupting the group's activity.

3. Address Disruptive Behaviors Immediately

- Ask to speak with the student privately in the hall, after class, or after school.
- Ask the student to explain what he thinks the problem is.
- Send "I messages" telling the student how his behavior affects you. For example, "I feel upset when I see you arguing with your group members."
- Try to identify the "real problem." Use the Problem-Solving Models to write down steps for trying to solve the problem (see Chapter 8).
- Draw up a social contract with the student to develop guidelines for future behavior (see Chapters 13 & 16).
- Monitor the student's behavior to give specific feedback.
- Encourage and praise students when they do well. "Catch Them Being Good."
- Renegotiate the social contract as needed.
- Prepare a modified case study to document chronic misbehaviors and to get outside help if needed (see Chapter 23).

Assignment

Use the following problem-solving strategy sheet to analyze the problem between Chuck and Mrs. Nordstrom in the chapter scenario or to solve a discipline problem of your own.

Problem-Solving Strategy

Student: _____ Date: _____ _____

Teacher: _____

Topic of Discussion: _____

Sense The Problem:

Identify the "Real" Problem:

(From *Blueprints for Thinking in the Cooperative Classroom*, Bellanca & Fogarty, 1991, p. 125.)

Brainstorm Ideas to Solve the Problem:

Prioritize Solutions: Rank

_____   _____

_____   _____

_____   _____

_____   _____

Sell Ideas to Others:

Plan the Action:

Face New Challenges:

Student's Signature _____

Teacher's Signature _____

(From *Blueprints for Thinking in the Cooperative Classroom*, Bellanca & Fogarty, 1991, p. 125)

 SKYLIGHT
PUBLISHING, INC.

SECTION
2
TEACHING COOPERATIVE SOCIAL SKILLS

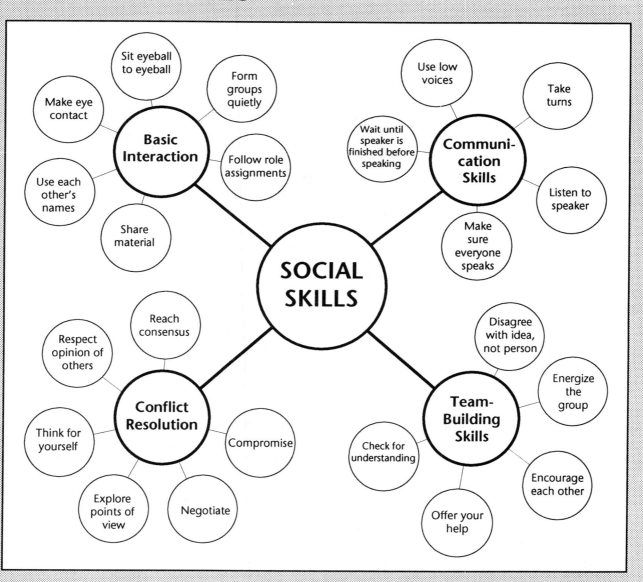

Teaching Cooperative Social Skills

It is sometimes said that moral concerns and social skills ought to be taught at home. I know of no one in the field of education or child development who disagrees. The problem is that such instruction—along with nurturance and warmth, someone to model altruism, opportunities to practice caring for others, and so forth—is not to be found in all homes. The school may need to provide what some children will not otherwise get. In any case, there is no conceivable danger in providing these values in both environments. (Kohn, 1991, p. 499)

Regardless of what teachers hope students have learned at home and in earlier grades, they still need to take the time to teach specific social skills to students. Students have been bombarded with "put-downs," "slams," or sarcasm masquerading as humor their whole lives. Many of their role models on television and in real life are people who get attention at the expense of somebody else's humiliation. Many students live in a family where "cutting down" their brothers and sisters and parents is commonplace. The fastest and wittiest person always seems to have the last laugh and ends up the "winner." Procedures, rules, and consequences form the organizational framework of classrooms, but the ultimate goal of educators should be to help students become responsible for their own actions and care for themselves and others.

The responsibility model of discipline provides students with opportunities to internalize good behavior and to treat others with respect because it is the right thing to do—not because it is a classroom rule! Kohn (1991) asks us to consider "the fact that most conversations about changing the way children act in a classroom tend to focus on curbing negative behaviors rather than on promoting positive ones" (p. 498).

Teaching cooperative social skills to students will help them develop interpersonal skills, self-esteem, and an internal locus of control. Responsible and caring students are more cooperative than irresponsible, non-caring students. A teacher's goal should be to provide the framework of a caring, cooperative classroom so that students begin to handle their own individual discipline problems, problems within their groups, and class-wide problems. Problem-solving, decision-making, and conflict-resolution skills should be taught, modeled, monitored, and re-taught as needed throughout the school year if students are expected to assume the responsibility for their own actions.

If teachers don't take the short time to re-educate students with positive social skills, they will spend a great deal of time "correcting" and "disciplining" disruptive students throughout the year. Bellanca (1991) states that a "well-conceived early childhood program ought to be saturated with social skill instruction and opportunity for the young students to practice as they play together" (p. ix). He says that the primary grades provide the best opportunity for students to develop the foundation of social skills, but the emphasis on skills must be continued in the middle grades and high school because that is where the peer pressure is strongest. Students need encouragement and support to ensure academic success and positive self-esteem. Bellanca, Fogarty, and others have suggested the following guidelines for teaching social skills.

STAGES IN TEACHING SOCIAL SKILLS
(Adapted from Bellanca, 1991)

1. **The hook or set.** This is a lesson that gets the students' attention and introduces the social skill.

   Example:

   Three students in a group role-play a discussion where everyone is arguing with each other. The students discuss a controversial issue like "drop-outs losing their driver's license," and emotions and tempers are out of control. Everyone is interrupting everyone else and voices are getting louder and angrier. After the role-play, members of the role-playing group comment on how they feel and on what specific actions or words upset them.

2. **Teach the skill.** Use a web or a T-chart to have students generate specific behaviors of the conflict-resolution skill of "Disagreeing with the idea—not the person."

   Disagreeing with the Idea—Not the Person

Sounds Like	Looks Like
"I hear what you are saying." "That's another way to look at it." "Please repeat that idea." "I have something to say when you're done." "Let's let Mary finish."	- Looking at the speaker - Taking notes - Nodding head - Not interrupting - Using a speaker's gavel when a person "has the floor"

   Complete the T-chart or web in groups or as a whole class and then post the charts on the bulletin board or have students keep a copy in their notebook to refer to whenever they engage in discussions.

3. **Practice.** Guided practice is necessary if students are to internalize the targeted social skill. Students select another controversial topic and discuss it in the group before presenting a consensus statement about the topic to the class. Group members give each other verbal and written feedback.

   Example:

   Topic: The district should adopt a "no pass; no play policy." Students who do not maintain an overall "C" average in school should not be able to participate in sports or other extracurricular activities.

Discussion: (10 minutes) Refer to T-chart on "Disagreeing with the idea—not the person."

Consensus Statement: The "no pass; no play" policy should not be adopted by the district because many students would drop out of school if they were not allowed to participate in extracurricular activities. Signed by the group members <u>Mary, Jose, Bryan</u>.

4. **Observation and feedback.** As students practice the targeted social skill, the teacher, a designated student observer, or the entire group should keep a checklist to monitor positive behaviors.

   Example:

Skill / Student	Looks at Speaker	Does not interrupt	Takes notes	Asks questions
Joe	X	X		X X X
Donna	X		X	
Mary Jo	X X			
Gail		X		

The group shares the results and the checklist serves as a formative assessment of what skills students need to practice. Practice should continue until the skill becomes automatic. Group members should encourage students who engage in a controversial discussion without getting angry, rude, or loud. Also, they should gently remind them when they speak while someone else is speaking or have a group symbol (magic marker, gavel, tennis ball) that the speaker holds and then passes on to the next speaker. Only the person with the symbol has the floor to speak.

5. **Reflection.** Students should reflect on their use of the social skill by discussing their use of the targeted skill, what they have learned about themselves and others, how much improvement they have made, and what they still need to do to improve even more. They

should also reflect on their group's implementation of the skills and discuss the group's progress.

Example:

Initial Observation	**Upon Reflection**
Date: <u>September 16</u>	**Date:** <u>September 25</u>
I always thought I kept my cool when I was in an argument, but my group members said I get red in the face and talk louder and faster when I want them to listen to me— I think I'm OK, but I'll try to be more careful.	After looking at our observer's checklist, I guess I *do* interrupt a lot—I guess I talk so fast that I can't sit still and listen to slower speakers—I'm going to have to be more patient and not try to "out talk" everyone else. I make people nervous.
	<div align="right">Kay</div>

6. **Recognition and Celebration.** As students internalize the social skills and practice them, they should receive recognition from their peers. The teacher and the peers can affirm positive behavior in specific terms like, "I like the way you asked me questions about my views on the subject." The group members can also devise a team signal or cheer to energize the group and encourage the members to celebrate their progress.

   Examples:
   • Group members give each other "high fives" after they finish a discussion where they respected each other's opinion.
   • The teacher selects one or two groups to present a debate to the class so students can demonstrate their use of the targeted social skill.
   • The whole class can engage in a discussion about a controversial topic and the teacher can monitor the social skill with an observation checklist.

7. **Transfer.** If students have really internalized the social skill, they should be able to transfer the skill outside of the classroom. If it is important to "disagree with the idea, not the person" in class, it should also be important to do the same thing on the playground, in the cafeteria, at the bus stop, in the neighborhood, and in the home.

Students should be encouraged to share their use of the skill outside the class with the group. After all, social skills are really life skills. Each week the base group could meet to discuss how members used the skill outside of class.

Example:

- Group members discuss how they utilize the targeted skill in everyday situations.
- Class members role-play situations that call for good discussion skills. Students could role-play a conversation between a son who received a bad report card and a father who wanted to "take away the car," or between an older conservative man and a young teenager about the merits of "rap" music or males wearing earrings.

The key component to social skills is to have the teacher and students decide what skills are important to learn in their class and why they are necessary for students to feel good about themselves and feel good about their peers. Students need to verbalize how they like to be treated before they can understand how they should treat others.

The following chapters will deal with four important facets of student responsibility and group interactions:

1. Basic Interactions
2. Communication Skills
3. Team-Building Skills
4. Conflict Resolution

Even though some of the skills are "self-evident," it is necessary to take the time to teach students social skills, to help them develop responsibility, and to enhance their self-esteem. Kohn (1991) says that "anyone interested in children as social beings must recognize the need to attend to the interactions among them in the classroom. In most American schools, children are forced to work either against one another (by competing) or apart from one another (by learning individually). The chance to work *with* one another, to learn social skills and caring, is left to happen by itself during recess, at lunch, or after school" (p. 503).

As most educators know, the choice to learn social skills and caring does not always happen by itself; it is the job of educators to help make it happen in the classroom so that, hopefully, it will happen outside the classroom as well.

Assignment

Complete the following by targeting a social skill and planning the lesson.

Stages in Teaching Social Skills

Target Social Skill: _____

Stage 1 – **The Hook or Set:**

Stage 2 – **Teach the Skill:**

Stage 3 – **Practice:**

Stage 4 – **Observation:**

Stage 5 – **Reflection:**

Stage 6 – **Recognition and Celebration:**

Stage 7 – **Transfer:**

4

Basic Interaction

"**G**ood morning class," says Mr. Parks as he greets his students.

"Today we will try something new. We will work in cooperative groups to solve our word problems in math. I'd like everyone to number off from one to eight—Ready? Tim you start..."

"Okay, now that you all have your numbers, I would like all the students with the same numbers to get into a group. The person who lives the farthest from school will be the organizer. The person who lives the next farthest will be the reporter. And the person who lives the closest to school will be the materials manager. Ready? Go!"

"Number three," yells Billy. *"Where are the other threes?"*

"Sixes," shouts Mary. *"Where are we going to sit?"*

"Over here," bellows Ann. *"Bring your desk over by me."*

"I can't find any two's, Mr. Parks. I think some people changed their numbers to go with their friends. I am all alone," Albert wails.

"What were we supposed to do?" whines Elizabeth. *"I don't know if I live the farthest or not, and if I did, what do I organize?"*

"What materials do I need?" shouts Sidney. *"And where are they?"*

"I still can't find my group," sobs Albert.

(10 minutes later...)

"Okay," says Mr. Parks. *"Now that everyone has found a group and figured out roles, we can begin our assignment."*

COOPERATIVE GROUP ACTIVITY

"Getting into groups" may seem like a basic social skill that all students from grades one to twelve could master in a few minutes of practice—right? Wrong! Every teacher has experienced the cacophony of desks banging against one other and students scattering in mass confusion. Getting into groups should take only a few minutes of precious class time; however, some classes spend as much as ten minutes just forming their groups, thus losing valuable time to accomplish their goals. Teachers at all grade levels should demonstrate to their classes the appropriate procedures. Working in cooperative groups is not just "working in groups." A great deal of preparation and training must precede the first attempt at cooperative learning.

How often have teachers said, "I tried cooperative learning with my students, but it just didn't work. This year I had a lot of kids with behavior problems and the students got too loud and nothing got done." After one or two unsuccessful forays into cooperative learning, many teachers simply abandon it and return to the traditional methods of teaching because students separated by rows of chairs are less likely to interact and make noise.

Cooperative group activities may fail if the teacher does not take the time to set up the groups properly. There are no shortcuts in the cooperative classroom. If time is not taken to set the climate for cooperation (bulletin boards, themes, bonding activities), to set up the procedures (how to get into groups, room arrangements, signals, assigned roles), to establish the groundwork (rules and consequences), and most importantly, to teach students social skills (listening, sharing, taking turns, helping one another) then the cooperative activity is doomed to failure.

A correlation could be made to the process of preparing student teachers or first-year teachers for their first teaching assignment. "Veteran" educators always warn the neophytes to be organized the first day of school. They warn the new teachers to establish procedures, rules, and consequences the first week of school so students know what is expected of them, and so that students know what will happen if they violate the rules.

Beginning teachers who don't establish expectations immediately because of the time involved and opt instead to talk about rules "as they see a need for them" often become disenchanted with their students early in the year. They find that they spend considerably more time throughout the year interrupting their lessons to address the same types of discipline problems over and over again. The frustration with the "time off task" and their "bad students" usually stretches throughout the entire year.

As veteran teachers have warned, it's a long, long, time from September to June, and once a class is out of control, it takes a long, long time (if ever) to get it back. *It is best to make the time at the beginning of the year to establish behavior and cooperative group guidelines. If this isn't done, teachers may find themselves having to take the time over and over again throughout the year to address behavior and group problems.*

Unfortunately, many students are not ready to learn and they do not know how to cooperate. It is important to identify what skills students need to know and take the time to teach them. Modeling appropriate behavior is an effective teaching method. Once students see what the appropriate behavior looks likes and sounds like and they see their teacher and fellow students modeling it, they will be more likely to internalize it themselves.

Some Cooperative Learning Basics

A good hook to introduce cooperative learning is to have the class complete a K-W-L sheet on cooperative learning. The students can list what they *Know* about cooperative learning in the first column; what they *Want* to know about cooperative learning in the second column. Later in the year, they can fill in the last column about what they *Learned* about cooperative learning (see p. 303 for blackline master).

Most experts in cooperative learning recommend waiting three or four weeks before assigning students to their heterogeneously mixed base groups. The base groups are composed of students of different races, sexes, and ability levels who will work together for as long as a quarter, semester, or year. Teachers need to get to know the students' ability levels, personalities, learning modalities, and behavior patterns first before assigning students to a base group.

It is essential that students be placed in base groups before they begin practicing the social skills. Students will be able to interact with all the students in the class during formal and informal group activities, but they should always return to their base group when specific social skills are introduced and taught.

Teachers who respect the dignity and individuality of students should allow the students to help formulate the rules and consequences that will govern group activities. If the classroom rules and consequences were decided by the class members at the beginning of the year, the students should be able to duplicate the process when it comes to determining group rules.

The teacher should call a class meeting to discuss cooperative learning and to tell the students about the philosophy behind cooperative groups, what their roles will be, and how the groups will function. The students should then brainstorm the types of roles the class will need and define the duties assigned for each of the roles.

Some possible roles include the following:

Organizer	Discussion Leader
Timekeeper	Observer
Materials Manager	Traveler
Recorder	Reader
Encourager	Praiser
Checker	Summarizer
Calculator	Keyboarder
Bookkeeper	Scout
Editor-in-Chief	Reporter

The students and the teacher should decide which roles will be most useful and then list the tasks of each of those roles. The following roles and duties could be used in cooperative groups in different classes and at different grade levels.

Example	
Roles	*Tasks*
Materials Manager	1. Finds out what materials are needed. 2. Makes sure everyone has what they need. 3. Returns materials after the activity.
Organizer	1. Assigns students their parts. 2. Watches time. 3. Makes sure all tasks are completed.
Recorder	1. Writes down what the group decides is important. 2. Reads ideas to group. 3. Checks for spelling and accuracy.
Encourager	1. Compliments group members. 2. Leads the group in a cheer. 3. Energizes the group.
Clarifier	1. Makes sure everyone understands the directions. 2. Checks for understanding. 3. Checks with other groups or teacher if no one in group understands.
Scout	1. Checks what other groups are doing. 2. Brings back information.
Editor-in-Chief	1. Assigns the members their work. 2. Makes sure the deadline is enforced. 3. Turns in the group's work.
Reporter	1. Makes sure he or she understands information. 2. Reports group ideas to class. 3. Answers questions.

SKYLIGHT PUBLISHING, INC.

After the roles and responsibilities have been established, students should brainstorm some cooperative group rules and some possible consequences if students do not function well in the groups. The teacher should initiate a class brainstorming session to elicit types of problems that could occur and write each problem on the board as students think of them.

Possible Cooperative Group Problems
1. Students who prefer to work alone
2. Students with whom no one wants to work
3. Students who talk all the time
4. Students who take over the group
5. Students who doodle or write notes to their friends
6. Students who are absent all the time
7. Students who don't have their work
8. Students who are sarcastic or use put-downs all the time

Activity #1

After the class has generated a list of possible problems, divide the members into groups of three or four, assign each group a specific problem, and ask the groups to brainstorm possible solutions using a web graphic organizer.

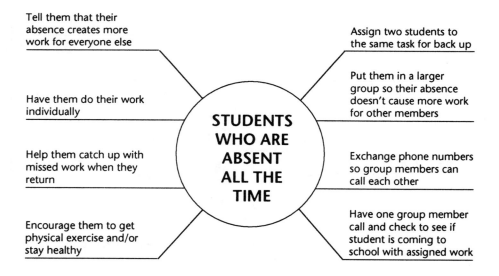

Activity #2

After each group has completed its web, share the ideas with the class. After the class has discussed all of the problems and possible solutions, vote on a list of possible consequences for each of the problems.

Sample Consequences
1. Group members discuss student's behavior with him or her.
2. Teacher talks to student about problem.
3. Student must talk with teacher and group members to discuss student's behavior before returning to group.
4. Student signs "social contract" describing what he or she will do to improve behavior (see Chapters 13 & 16).

Because students are individuals, a prescribed formula does not fit all situations. Make it very clear that the teacher always reserves the right to select or alter the consequences depending on individual students and cases. Through this exercise, students become aware of the types of problems that might occur in group situations, and more importantly, they become aware of how their peers feel about specific behaviors.

Sometimes, however, the teacher must deal with a specific problem that one student is having with the whole class. For example, if class members are continuously making fun of a student, the teacher may have to send the student on an errand so he or she can discuss the situation with the group or the entire class. Everyone in the class must be treated with dignity and respect.

Assignment

Brainstorm a list of possible solutions to the problem of students who forget to bring their work.

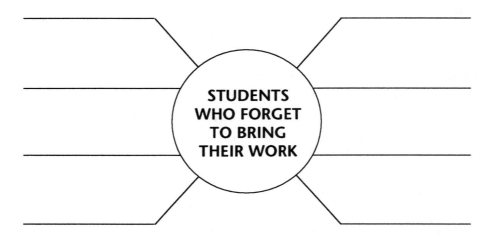

Select another problem students might have in cooperative groups and brainstorm possible solutions to the problem.

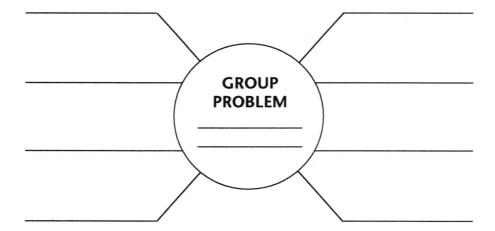

SOCIAL SKILLS
Basic Interaction

Form Groups Quietly

Sit Eyeball to Eyeball

Make Eye Contact

Use Each Other's Names

Share Materials

Follow Role Assignments

SKYLIGHT PUBLISHING, INC.

5

Communication Skills

"**S**hut up!" yells Martha as she leaps up from her desk. *"You don't know what you are talking about!"*

"Yes, I do," screams Jose. *"You just never give me a chance to talk because you are always talking so much!"*

"Martha, Jose! What's going on here? Why are you yelling? You are disturbing all the other groups."

"But Mrs. Green," Martha whines, *"I am sick and tired of Jose mouthing off about something he doesn't know anything about. He never takes turns."*

"Okay, Martha and Jose. I am going to let you two work this problem out," Mrs. Green says. *"I am going to take the roll and check homework for a few minutes, but I'll be back!"*

"You jerk. Now you got us in trouble. I need another partner," mutters Martha.

"You need a muzzle," laughs Jose. *"Your mouth is never shut."*

THE NEED TO PRACTICE

Students need to practice communicating with one another. One way to emphasize important skills in this area is to have each base group complete a T-chart on listening skills. Listing specific things people say and do when they are listening is more concrete and memorable than having the teacher yell out, "Now listen," every five minutes.

The following activities are designed as hooks, teaching methods for social skills, guided practice, observations, and reflections for introducing the social skills that improve communication within cooperative groups.

HOOK

Fishbowl

One activity to "hook" students is to use a "fishbowl" technique. Ask two students to move their desks into the center of the room so everyone in the class can see them (thus, the fishbowl effect). Ask them to role-play a typical conversation. Call one student aside and tell him to talk about an interesting place he went or something fun he did that really excited him. Call the other student aside and ask her privately *not* to listen to the speaker. In other words, to demonstrate inattentive listening strategies. Ask the other students in the classroom to observe the two carefully. After the activity, ask the speaker how he felt about the conversation. Then ask the speaker and the rest of the class to use a T-chart to list what non-listening "sounded like" and "looked like." Complete the T-chart in groups and then share the characteristics by creating one unduplicated list on a big piece of paper for the class.

T-Chart: Non-Listening

LESSON

Sounds Like	Looks Like
tapping pencil	darting eyes
winding watch	fidgeting
saying "uh huh" a lot	playing with hair
saying "really"	putting on lipstick
sighing	going through folder
asking unrelated questions	looking down
making inappropriate	turning away
comments	not facing speaker

Once the class has listed all their ideas, tear up the list and put it in the trash to symbolize that the groups and the class will not tolerate non-listening habits.

Have two more student volunteers act out good listening skills in a fishbowl role-playing activity. Following this activity, the whole class can then brainstorm ideas for the "Attentive Listening T-Chart."

T-Chart: Attentive Listening

Sounds Like	Looks Like
positive feedback	Nodding
"Tell me that again."	Making eye contact
"I know what you mean."	Sitting eye to eye,
"Tell us more."	knee to knee
"What you're saying is…"	Positive body language

LESSON

This list should be posted in the room to remind everyone of the importance of listening to others. Often teachers can come near a "non-listening" student during a group activity and merely point to the "Attentive Listening Poster" as a gentle reminder of the exemplary characteristics expected from all the group members.

T-Chart: Making Sure Everyone Speaks

Sounds Like	Looks Like
"Okay, now it's your turn."	Smiling
"Who haven't we heard from?"	Nodding
"We haven't heard from Doug yet."	Eye contact with speaker
"Let's rotate speaking."	Speaker's symbol (magic marker, token) passed around so that only one person speaks at a time
	Checker keeps track of who speaks
	Group uses positive gestures

LESSON

Round Robin Listening Circle

Another activity that emphasizes good listening is the "Round Robin Listening Circle." Assign three students to a group. The roles will rotate so that each person gets a turn to be the speaker, the listener, and the observer. Assign a controversial topic or give the group a controversial article to read. Tell the speaker that he or she has five minutes to discuss the topic with the listener. The listener can respond during the time to simulate a regular conversation. The observer takes notes on what the listener is doing and saying.

At the end of the five-minute round, the observer shares feedback with the listener. The roles then rotate, and the same procedure is used. It is important to "process" each round by asking the observers what they observed so that students can be aware of things they do and say that might demonstrate poor listening traits.

Some thought-provoking topics students might use are:
1. The effects of secondary smoke on non-smokers.
2. Students who don't pass all their classes cannot participate in extracurricular activities.
3. Taking away the driver's license of dropouts.
4. Requiring all students to do volunteer work in their community.
5. Allowing students to go off campus for lunch.

Have the students reflect on their own listening ability and ask them if they listen better when they *agree* with the speaker. Often people who *disagree* with a speaker do not listen as well because they are so busy thinking of rebuttals.

Processing the Use of Social Skills

Individual students and groups can reflect on their use of the targeted social skill by using some of the following strategies:

1. Rating scales for how well they used the skill

   a.   Social Skill: _____

   /——/——/——/——/——/——/——/——/——/——/
   0   5   10

b. How well did we do?

Slow Start	Gaining Momentum	Won The Race
	Indy 500 of Social Skills	

GROUP REFLECTION

2. PMI Chart. Analyze the group's use of a social skill.

P (Pluses)	M (Minuses)	I (Interesting Points)

GROUP REFLECTION

3. Reflective Log or Journal

Reflective Log On (Social Skill)_____

Initial Observation	*Upon Reflection*
Date:_____	Date:_____

Signed:_____

INDIVIDUAL REFLECTION

4. Group Observation Checklist

Group Member	Skill	Feedback Symbol
Mary	Taking Turns	√
	Listening	√+
	Encouraging	–
	Staying on Task	√

GROUP
REFLECTION

5. Reflective Questions for Group Work

What were we supposed to do?

What did we do well?

What would we do differently next time?

Do we need any help?

Activity #1

Select one of the following processing methods and have students use it to analyze how well their group has done on learning and using a social skill.

• Rating scales

• PMI Chart

• Reflective Log

• Group Observation Checklist

• Reflective Questions

Activity #2

1. Select three controversial topics and distribute short articles on these topics to all of the students to read.

2. Assign students to groups of three. Select one of the controversial topics and assign a speaker to talk about the topic for three minutes. Assign a listener to listen and give feedback to the speaker. Assign an observer to take notes on the checklist.

3. After the three minutes are up, ask the observer to give specific feedback to the listener.

4. Process the observer's comments with the entire class.

5. Select another controversial topic and rotate the roles.

6. Begin the procedure again.

Round Robin Listening Circle

Topic: _____   Time Limit: _____

Speaker: _____

Listener: _____

Observer: _____

The speaker should start the round by giving his or her opinion on the topic, but the listener should join in the conversation and respond to the speaker's opinion. The observer should take notes on what the listener says and does by making comments or making checks every time a behavior is observed.

Observation of the Listener

Put a "✓" each time a behavior occurs and write down specific observations.

Listener: _____

	CHECKS	COMMENTS
Giving Feedback	_____	_____
Asking Questions	_____	_____
Paraphrasing	_____	_____
Body Language	_____	_____
Facial Expressions	_____	_____
Other	_____	_____

Assignment

Develop your own original processing method to assess students' communication skills.

SOCIAL SKILLS
Communication

Use Low Voices

Take Turns

Make Sure Everyone Has a Turn to Speak

Listen to the Speaker

Wait Until Speaker is Finished Before You Speak

SKYLIGHT
PUBLISHING, INC.

6

Team-Building Skills

"**O**h no!" Paul says, near tears. *"I've lost my entire research paper—I can't believe I deleted it. Four weeks of work!"*
"Relax, Paul, you can get it back on the screen. Just read the manual and it will tell you how. Be patient," says Pete.
"I hate computers. I'll never learn all this stuff!" Paul says, frantically searching through the manual.

"Don't worry—you'll figure it out," says Pete.

"You shouldn't spend time on my problem, Pete. You have your own paper to finish and it's due tomorrow."

"That's okay, Paul. That's what group members are for."

"Wow, I found the file! It wasn't deleted. It was just off the screen." Paul says, relieved.

"Thanks for helping me. I would have been in big trouble!"

BONDING

The concept of team building is critical to the success of cooperative groups. Even though taking the time from the "content" and the "textbook" to practice bonding activities to build trust and rapport may seem frivolous to some, its importance can not be emphasized enough.

Bonding activities allow students in a group to know each other better by discovering common likes and dislikes, similar hobbies, talents, tastes, and other things that make for lasting friendships. It is important to forge friendships in all group activities, but it is essential when it comes to forming base groups. The following bonding activities will help bring students closer to their fellow group members and make them more willing to give help, encouragement, and support.

Activity #1—True-False Quiz

1. Pair two students in the group and give them ten minutes each to interview each other. Encourage them to ask lots of "far out" or creative questions so the class can get to know the real person.

2. After the students have interviewed their partners, tell them to construct a five-item, true-or-false quiz about their partners. Make sure to include questions that could stump the rest of the class.

3. Have students introduce their partners to the class and read the questions aloud. The class will vote "True" or "False" on each question.

Example:

1-Mike has just returned from a visit to his uncle in Australia.	T	F
2-Mike's favorite singer is Bruce Springsteen.	T	F
3-Mike loves writing research papers.	T	F
4-Mike's mom is a former Miss America.	T	F
5-Mike has won five tennis trophies.	T	F

4. After the class votes on each question, then the partner will tell the right answer and a little bit about the question.

Example:

Question 4: Mike's mother is a former Miss America.   T   F

The answer is "False." In fact, Mike's mother went to Atlantic City last year to protest the pageant.

Students have fun with the quiz, and it is a good way to get to know something intriguing about the students without requiring them to give a speech about themselves. This activity can also be used with groups of three, but it takes longer to make sure all three students are interviewed so that each group member can introduce one of the other members to the group.

Activity #2—The Venn and the Triple Venn

This activity works for two, three, or four people in a base group. If there are four students, put them in pairs and have each pair complete a Venn diagram stating how they are different and how they are alike. Groups of three can do a triple Venn. Use big newsprint or transparencies so the Venns can be shared with the entire class. Students feel more comfortable introducing each other when they have the graphic organizer to help them.

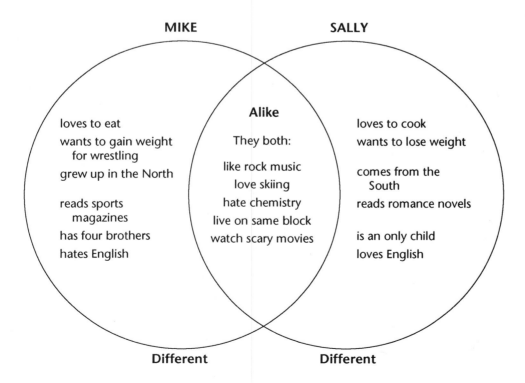

MIKE   SALLY

loves to eat
wants to gain weight
   for wrestling
grew up in the North

reads sports
   magazines
has four brothers
hates English

Alike

They both:

like rock music
love skiing
hate chemistry
live on same block
watch scary movies

loves to cook
wants to lose weight

comes from the
   South
reads romance novels

is an only child
loves English

Different   Different

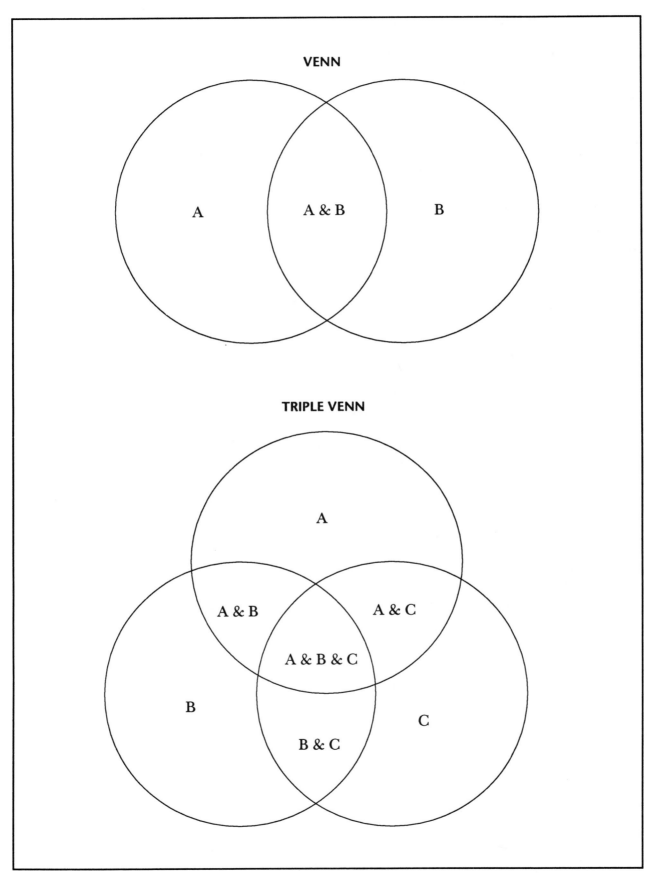

VENN

A | A & B | B

TRIPLE VENN

A

A & B | A & C

A & B & C

B | B & C | C

SKYLIGHT PUBLISHING, INC.

Activity #3—Create a Business

1. Have each student in the base group write down a list of all his or her strengths. Make sure they include everything they do well (sports, gardening, artwork, talking, handwriting, etc.).
2. Share the lists with the groups.
3. See if any strengths appear several times.
4. Based on the strengths of the team members, invent a business your team could start.
5. Name the business.
6. Devise a business card you can use.
7. Write a television or radio commercial advertising your business.
8. Design a logo, ad, or billboard for your business.
9. Write a poem, jingle, song, or rap song to advertise it.
10. Share your ideas with the entire class.

Activity #4—Creative Energizers

It is amazing how close students will become once they have gone through a risk-taking ordeal together. Even though some older students will look at the teacher like he or she is crazy, deep down many of them relish the idea of acting out their musical, poetic, or creative talents to an audience of their peers.

Each base group should be assigned a presentation to make in front of the class. After the group has a chance to talk, get to know one another, and discover each other's likes and dislikes, they are ready for the bonding activity. They need to decide on a group name based on their personalities, come up with a motto, and create a sign with their group logo. They then must select two of the following items to present to the class:

1. A poem depicting the group's goals, expectations, fears, etc.
2. A cheer that epitomizes their team spirit.
3. A TV commercial that depicts the outstanding merits of the group.
4. A rap song that describes themselves in musical verse.
5. A radio jingle advertising their unity.
6. A group dance or cheer.
7. An ad that captures the essence of the group spirit.
8. A pantomime that symbolizes togetherness.

They must also create an "energizer" or sign of encouragement the members will use when their entire group or one of their members does something well. Creativity and originality are encouraged, but the list below contains some common ones created by Michelle Borba (1990) and others that they could adopt. Students need to celebrate when they do a good job using their social skills, and recognition from their peers is probably more effective in building self-esteem than a token or certificate from their teacher.

"Energizers"

1. High-five sign (two people raise one hand and clap them together)
2. Thumbs-up sign
3. "Uh-huh, Uh-huh" (point fingers at person being honored)
4. "Right-on, baby"
5. "Round" of applause (students clap their hands while moving them in a circle in front of them)
6. Standing or sitting "O" for "ovation"—students form circle with arms over their heads
7. Air Guitar—"Excellent" (pretend to play a guitar and say "Excellent")
8. "Yes!" (pull one arm in at side and say "Yes!"; double "Yes!"—pull other arm down on other side; triple "Yes!"—pull both arms down the middle)
9. "Yo *uh-huh*" (put hands over head in circle and then do Egyptian sign to both sides)
10. Artic Shiver (wave hands in air without making noise)
11. Hand-jive (be creative)
12. The wave (students start wave on one side of the room)
13. "Awesome" cheer (raise hands up in air, then lower and raise them slowly whispering in a hushed voice—"Awesome")

The students will share their signal with the class, and the teacher will tell groups when they are allowed to reward and honor other class members with their official seal of approval.

Students enjoy receiving praise and encouragement from each other and sometimes the traditional "smattering" of applause just does not convey a true sense of appreciation or excitement. The group energizer will "personalize" their recognition and encourage their continued participation. Students and adults love recognition and encouragement, and receiving attention from one's peers motivates and stimulates positive interaction.

Having students evaluate their own behavior, social skills, and group work is part of Glasser's Quality School concept. He feels that students should evaluate their own work for quality to see how satisfying quality can be. When students appraise their own performance and assess the quality of their own work, they are well on the way to becoming self-sufficient and responsible adults.

Assignment

Brainstorm another activity that would encourage students to bond with other group members.

SOCIAL SKILLS
Team-Building Skills

Check for Understanding

Offer Your Help

Ask Your Group First for Help if You Don't Understand

Encourage Each Other

Energize the Group

Disagree with the Idea—Not the Person

SKYLIGHT PUBLISHING, INC.

7

Conflict Resolution

"**Y**eah, right, Sarah," Jack says. "*What kind of idiot would ever consider voting democratic. Are you crazy?*"

"*Jack,*" Rose implores. "*We are supposed to be working on a Venn diagram comparing one Republican candidate with one Democratic candidate. Don't get hysterical.*"

"*I'm just amazed that someone is stupid enough to ever consider Sarah's candidate.*"

"*Thanks for listening, Jack,*" Sarah says sarcastically, "*I really appreciate your open mind and willingness to listen. You're such a supportive group member.*"

"*Well, you don't know anything about the candidates,*" says Jack. "*You are just voting the way your parents vote!*"

"*I am not going to sit here and listen to that know-it-all analyze my life,*" Sarah says with emotion.

"*Okay you guys. We need to finish this assignment,*" interrupts Rose. "*You two need to cool it.*"

HANDLING CONFLICT

Contrary to the beliefs of many teachers, students should be encouraged to disagree and argue with each other. Teachers who spend time bonding the groups and getting them to conform often become upset when the group members begin to engage in disagreements or express opposite points of view. Introducing controversial topics into a lesson is often discouraged because the arguments may cause discipline problems. However, controversy should be encouraged because it leads to higher-order thinking skills and higher-level social skills.

C.R.

The key is not to avoid conflicts, but to teach students how to handle them. The social skills related to conflict resolution need to be taught, retaught, reviewed, and taught again until they are embedded in the students. Everyone knows of people who possess many other wonderful social skills, but their inability to listen and respect others' opinions or reach agreement on any divisive issue often causes them immeasurable problems in their personal and professional lives. Students should be taught how to engage in controversy or conflict by listening to others' ideas, respecting their opinions, and learning how to disagree with the idea—not the person.

These social skills are especially important for students in gifted programs. Exceptionally intelligent students may be the center of attention and dominate other students because of their abilities. These same students, however, may not function well in cooperative groups unless they are "in charge." They may become withdrawn or angry when everyone else does not want to go along with their plan.

C.R

In the course of these discussions, students will disagree with each other; but if students have internalized the social skills that go along with conflict resolution, they will know how to disagree with the idea without alienating the person. They will also develop the critical thinking skills that help them to listen to the opinions of others, to analyze a problem by examining all sides, to form an intelligent opinion, and to persuade people to agree with them.

C.L

One of the goals of cooperative learning is to help students make decisions. If students are to achieve this goal, they need to be exposed to people who think differently than they do and to ideas that are contrary to their beliefs. Learning how to formulate and to defend one's beliefs rationally, intelligently, and calmly in a multi-ethnic society is an important life skill. Students need to be prepared to live in a society where opinions are as diverse as the population and where controversy exists in the classroom, community, nation, and world. Being able to see different points of view, negotiate, and compromise are essential life skills.

The following activities encourage students to form and defend opinions within the framework of trust, respect, and courtesy.

Activity #1—Agree/Disagree Chart

1.   Introduce the Agree/Disagree Graphic Organizer chart (see p. 286 for blackline master). Students are to note that the chart has a BEFORE column and an AFTER column. They are to use the BEFORE column before the activity or lesson, and the AFTER column after the activity or lesson. Prior to studying a topic, distribute copies of the chart and ask each group Reader to read the statements out loud. Ask the Recorder to write the names of each group member under either the Agree or Disagree column, according to their opinion about each statement.

2.   Study the topic, listen to a lecture, view a film, read an article, attend an assembly, read a book, or go on a field trip.

3.   Have the group Readers read each of the statements again. The team members should think about the statements in light of the new information they have received, and then write their name in the AFTER column of the Agree/Disagree Chart.

4.   Students should be encouraged to discuss their views with the other team members.

5.   The following example of a unit on "Chemical Dependency" could be used prior to a unit on drugs and alcohol and then again after the unit.

Agree/Disagree Chart
Alcohol Drug Unit

Statement	Before		After	
	Agree	Disagree	Agree	Disagree
1. Marijuana is a safe drug.		Jose Mary Dave Monica		Jose Mary Dave Monica
2. Alcoholism is a disease.	Dave	Jose Mary Monica	Jose Mary Dave	Monica
3. Coffee can reduce alcohol in the body.	Jose Mary Dave Monica			Jose Mary Dave Monica
4. Men can drink more than women.	Jose Mary	Dave Monica		Jose Mary Dave Monica
5. Steroids are legal in pro sports.		Jose Mary Dave Monica		Jose Mary Dave Monica
6. Crack is not as lethal as cocaine.	Mary Dave	Jose Monica		Jose Mary Dave Monica
7. Heroine is always addictive.	Jose Mary Dave Monica		Jose Dave	Mary Monica
8. Alcoholism runs in families; it's in the genes	Jose Dave	Mary Monica	Mary Dave	Jose Monica

(Chart from *Patterns for Thinking: Patterns for Transfer* by Robin Fogarty and James Bellanca, Skylight Publishing, Palatine, IL, 1987.)

Activity #2—Consensus Chart

1. Assign students the task of coming up with their group's top three television shows.

2. Have the Recorder write down ten programs from the titles that the group members brainstorm.

3. In order to help reach consensus, have the groups take a "reading" of each person's rating of the television shows by doing a "five to fist" as the title is announced. (*This is not a vote!*)

4. If a student holds up a fist, he or she must provide an alternative title.

5. Students who want a show on the list can try to persuade other students who show two fingers (let's talk more) or three fingers (okay with me) to agree with the choice.

6. The consensus cycle of Talk-Discuss-Persuade-Justify should be used until the group can reach consensus on the top three shows.

Activity #3—The Human Graph

1. Select several controversial topics before engaging in the human graph experiment. Topics might include the following:
   - Making school year twelve months long instead of nine
   - Uniforms for all public school students
   - Raising the driving age to eighteen
   - Revoking driver's licenses of students who drop out of school
   - Requiring all high school students to complete sixty hours of community service as part of their graduation requirements
   - Requiring all students who participate in extracurricular activities (sports, clubs, bands, etc.) to maintain an overall "C" average and earn no grade lower than a "D" in any class
   - Requiring all students to take at least one foreign language

2. Make a statement about the topic. For example, the teacher might say, "All public school students should be required to wear uniforms to school."

Stand in the middle of the room to indicate the "neutral position." Students in favor of the statement stand to the right of the teacher; students opposed stand to the left. The position they take indicates how strongly they feel about the topic.

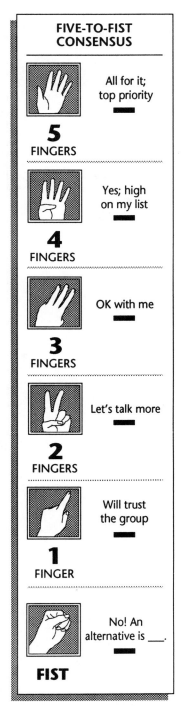

FIVE-TO-FIST CONSENSUS

5 FINGERS — All for it; top priority

4 FINGERS — Yes; high on my list

3 FINGERS — OK with me

2 FINGERS — Let's talk more

1 FINGER — Will trust the group

FIST — No! An alternative is ___.

(From *Blueprints for Thinking in the Cooperative Classroom* by James Bellanca and Robin Fogarty, Skylight Publishing ©1991)

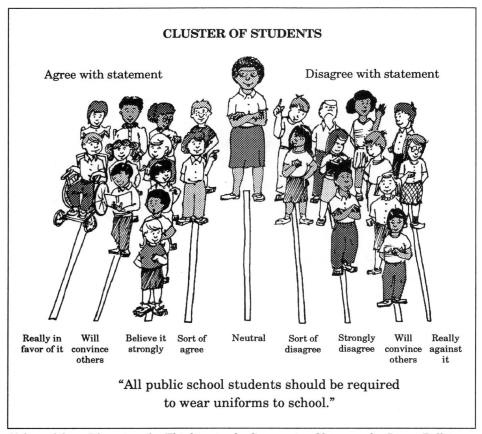

CLUSTER OF STUDENTS

Agree with statement   Disagree with statement

| Really in favor of it | Will convince others | Believe it strongly | Sort of agree | Neutral | Sort of disagree | Strongly disagree | Will convince others | Really against it |

"All public school students should be required
to wear uniforms to school."

(Adapted from *Blueprints for Thinking in the Cooperative Classroom* by James Bellanca
and Robin Fogarty, Skylight Publishing, © 1991.)

3.   Students can line up in front of one another if they share the same opinions.

4.   Students can remain neutral in front of the teacher if they don't know anything about the topic or if they don't have an opinion.

5.   Call on students to explain why they feel the way they do about the topic. Only one person speaks at a time.

6.   Everyone listens to all arguments.

7.   After several students have expressed their opinions, give a signal to allow everyone to change positions in the human graph to represent their changed opinions on the topic.

8.   Ask students why they changed their opinions.

The activity allows for a great deal of interaction and it allows students to use their facts and ideas to persuade others to side with their view. It also emphasizes effective listening skills and the importance of keeping an open mind. Students often change their position, literally and figuratively, by listening to arguments and reassessing their stance on a topic.

Activity #4—Conflict Resolution

1. Explain the roles of Court Reporter, Judge, and Bailiff to the cooperative teams. The Court Reporter will write down all the group's ideas on the team sheet. The Judge will (a) make sure each team member agrees, and (b) explain the team's ideas to the class. The Bailiff will (a) make sure the team finishes on time, and (b) look up words in the dictionary.

2. Assign roles by alphabetical order. The person in the group whose first name comes first in the alphabet will be the Court Reporter; the second person will be the Judge; and the third person will be the Bailiff.

3. Ask the Bailiff to read the rules of working together in the courtroom to your group.

Rules for Working Together
   a. Listen carefully to all arguments.
   b. One person talks at a time.
   c. Stay with the team.
   d. Do your job well.
   e. Be positive.
   f. Tell the truth; you are under oath.

4. Remind the Court Reporter to have the team's dictionary ready.

5. Ask the students to look over the following checklist. Tell them to discuss each of the words listed and make sure everyone in the group understands the definitions. They are to check off each word after everyone understands it.

What Do You Do When You Disagree?
   - ❑ *Argue*—repeat the same ideas and stand firm
   - ❑ *Persuade*—justify, provide reasons to back up your ideas or appeal to emotion
   - ❑ *Vote*—count votes to select the majority
   - ❑ *Compromise*—combine, modify ideas
   - ❑ *Mediate*—find a neutral party facilitator to judge
   - ❑ *Arbitrate*—agree to abide by decision of an assigned person who takes best from both sides
   - ❑ *Delay*—table it, sleep on it, wait
   - ❑ *Reconceptualize*—rethink, find new angles
   - ❑ *Negotiate*—give and take
   - ❑ *Give in*—give up, cave in, play martyr

❑ *Seek Consensus*—talk, juggle, adjust, modify, find agreement for sides to "live with"

❑ *Humor*—veer away from confrontation

❑ *Avoid*—ignore or postpone indefinitely

(Bellanca & Fogarty, 1991, p. 139)

6. Have each person in the group select one of the strategies for conflict resolution listed above and tell about a time when he or she used that strategy effectively.

7. Now have them rank order the three strategies their group feels are most effective for solving conflicts.

#1 Strategy   _____

#2 Strategy   _____

#3 Strategy   _____

Assignment

1. Fill out the Agree/Disagree Chart with controversial true/false statements about conflict resolution (see blackline, p. 286). Get together with a group of colleagues and fill out the chart together.

2. Fill out an Agree/Disagree chart with controversial true/false statements about a topic you would teach to your students. Give the chart to groups of students to complete both before and after the unit.

SOCIAL SKILLS
Conflict Resolution

Disagree with the Idea—Not the Person

Respect the Opinion of Others

Think for Yourself

Explore Different Points of View

Negotiate and/or Compromise

Reach Consensus

SKYLIGHT PUBLISHING, INC.

Part

The Challenges

SECTION

3

STUDENTS WHO HAVE TROUBLE ACCEPTING RESPONSIBILITY

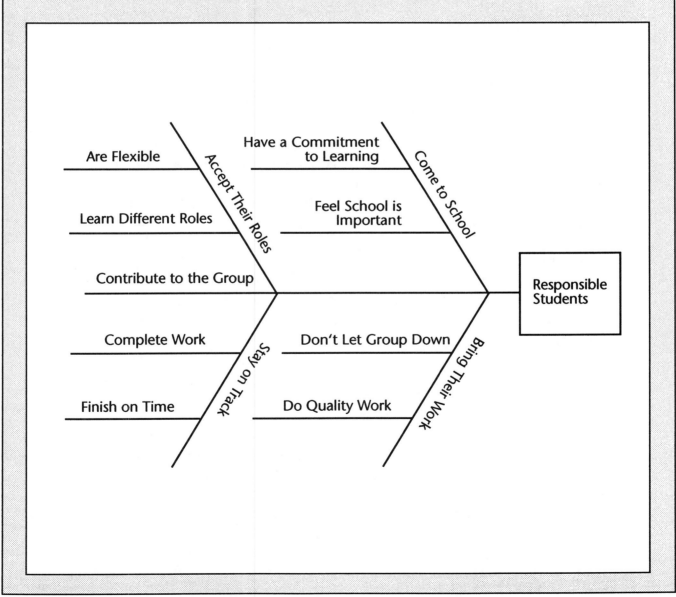

Students Who Have Trouble Accepting Responsibility

When students are upset, they are never responsible; they are always victims of someone who has caused their misery. (Glasser, 1986, p. 47)

Many students have trouble accepting responsibility for their own actions and choose instead to blame other students, their teacher, their parents, the "system," the society, or any number of external forces for their own problems.

The first problems students encounter often start in the early grades when they begin to avoid responsibility by staying home from school. Absenteeism in students is evident as early as kindergarten. The same students repeatedly come late to school because they don't feel well or they oversleep. These students also tend to get sick during the day and have to go to the office to rest or have a parent pick them up. This pattern of behavior continues into early grade school where the student rotates between absences and making up work—never really establishing a routine or developing the sense of responsibility necessary for success. Unfortunately, many parents contribute to the pattern of irresponsibility without realizing the long-term detrimental effects. Many teachers, however, know the damaging effects absences can have on students' development of social skills, academic skills, and responsibility skills, and how difficult it becomes to "make up" the work and catch up with the rest of the class.

A recent study confirms teachers' feelings and shows that an early record of absenteeism could be an indicator of later failure in school. Superintendent Douglas Hoeft and his staff in Kane County, Illinois (cited in Kendall, 1990) conducted a study that found that a vast majority of students who dropped out of high school had missed a large number of school days during the first few years of their education. Hoeft and his staff analyzed records from the area high schools and compared the students' academic success with their attendance records since kindergarten. The study found that when compared with dropouts, the students who graduated in the top twenty-five percent of their high school class had missed about one-third as many days of school in kindergarten, and about one-half as many days in the first through the third grades. The study showed a direct correlation between early absenteeism and later difficulty in school. "As Captain Kangaroo once noted, kids don't drop out of high school, they drop out of kindergarten, then they wait 10 years to make it official" (Kendall, 1990).

Children develop their attendance patterns, their love or hate relationship with school, and their own self-concepts very early. If school provides them with a positive environment, if school is satisfying to them, and if they feel good about themselves and what they accomplish, then students will become responsible learners. Students will want to attend school more if they know that they will be treated with respect, that they will be liked by their teachers and peers, and that they will feel good about themselves.

How can teachers set the tone for a positive climate that helps students feel comfortable? Researchers such as Dreikurs, Grunwald, and Pepper (1980); Dinkmeyer, McKay, and Dinkmeyer (1980); and Collis and Dalton (1990) have stressed the importance of establishing an encouraging environment for all students.

What Teachers Can Do to Establish an Encouraging Environment for All Students

1. Cue students by using their first name prior to talking to them or giving them a task.
2. Be organized. Students need clear rules and procedures.
3. Establish eye contact, but be aware of cultural differences that may make prolonged direct eye contact threatening.
4. Work at students' physical level when talking with them one-on-one (don't stand over students and look down on them).
5. Stand or sit close to students when addressing them or monitoring them (don't shout across the room).

6. Develop a personalized way of cuing students who have chronic discipline problems (e.g., a slight tap on the shoulder, a special look, a "T" signal for time-out, or a signal that shows the student has "crossed the line").
7. Reinforce good behavior.
8. Encourage—Encourage—Encourage!
9. Handle all disruptions as privately and confidentially as possible.
10. Provide feedback and follow-up for all conferences, social contracts, or behavior plans. (Collis & Dalton, 1990)

Collis and Dalton (1990, p. 19) describe the three types of classroom leadership.

Teacher Ownership	**Shared Ownership**	**Student Ownership**
• Strong teacher control	• Shared control	• strong student control
• "I decide what you will do."	• "Let's decide together."	• "You decide what you will do."
• External control based on authority	• The teacher invites:	• Internal control based on self-direction

• Teacher makes decisions and choices	- input
	  - negotiation
	  - responsibility
	  - cooperation
	  and helps children learn the appropriate skills for becoming responsible learners.
		• "I'm responsible for my learning."

• Teacher is responsible for learning.	• Children are learning both independence and interdependence.	• Children are independent of the teacher
• Children are dependent on the teacher.	• "I am responsible for my learning and I care about the learning of others."	

Teachers can use all three styles of leadership according to the situation; however, the "shared ownership" style is best for helping students learn the skills necessary for them to become responsible learners.

Students need to be taught responsibility just like they need to be taught social skills. Effective teachers can help students take responsibility for their actions by trying to meet students' individual learning needs before group assignments are made. Structuring the activities so that all students will be successful and providing reflection and feedback on all activities are helpful techniques.

One vital component of teaching students responsibility involves the use of encouragement. Purkey (1971) and many others have pointed out that students' learning achievement is related to their self-concept and expectations. Students who are constantly discouraged by their peers, parents, or teachers will believe themselves to be poor learners or "losers" and will perform according to their low expectations. Unfortunately, many students develop these low expectations about themselves at a very early age, and their low self-concept sometimes becomes a self-fulfilling prophecy.

Teachers play a vital role in determining whether or not a student is encouraged or discouraged. If the teacher models positive encouragement and embeds it in the social skills taught to all students, and if the teacher monitors those skills throughout the year, then he or she will create a positive and caring classroom atmosphere that is conducive to learning.

One way teachers can foster this positive encouragement is to practice effective listening. Dinkmeyer and Losoncy (1980) draw the following distinctions between effective and ineffective listening.

Ineffective listening	**Effective listening**
Focuses on negatives	Focuses on positives
Competing, comparing	Cooperative
Threatening	Accepting
Uses sarcasm, embarrassment	Uses humor, hope
Humiliates	Stimulated
Recognizes only well-done tasks	Recognizes effort and improvement
Disinterested in feelings	Interested in feelings
Bases worth on performance	Bases worth on just being

(Dinkmeyer, & Losoncy, 1980, p. 6)

Encouraging listeners listen to students without making judgments or accusations. They also resist the temptation to send "you-messages" that accuse, blame, or criticize and are usually accompanied by a sarcastic or disrespectful tone.

> "Quiet down!"
> "The groups are too loud!"
> "That's it. It's too noisy. Put your desks back in rows."

These statements all imply the word "you" and they become ultimatums issued from an authority figure (Gordon, 1974). Students often feel embarrassed, put down, or angry when teachers send "you-messages," making them less likely to want to cooperate. Also, some students equate statements about their actions with their self-worth and become defensive.

"You-messages" often do not work because students who always hear, "You're wrong," "Why can't you remember to bring your homework?" and "Why can't you get along with others?" may begin to believe their behavior really reflects their personality. If this happens, students typically either fulfill the prophecy of their own failure or they refuse to accept the blame and act out to show their rebellion.

When teachers use "I-messages," however, they appeal to students' good nature and spirit of cooperation. When teachers say things like "I'm upset," or "I am very concerned about your grades," they take responsibility for their own feelings and at the same time leave the students to worry about their own behavior.

Students are often surprised when they hear teachers express personal feelings or concerns without placing blame on the students. The key to successful "I-messages," however, lies in sincerity, tone of voice, and depth of feelings. "I-messages laced with anger (or with similar hostile feelings like annoyance, hurt, disgust) have the same effect as you-messages" (Dinkmeyer, McKay, and Dinkmeyer, 1980, p. 99). When teachers are too angry to approach the student coolly and calmly, they should wait to address the problem or they should delay their reaction until they are calm. If teachers give encouragement and positive feedback, they will show they recognize effort and improvement, value self-evaluation, allow students to be imperfect, and challenge students to be willing to try new ideas and take risks.

"Responsibility" is not something teachers require students to bring to school the first week along with their notebook, supplies, and immunization records! Students need to develop responsibility as early as kindergarten and practice it throughout school. One of the major goals of the business world is to hire responsible workers. Students who are not taught to be responsible for their learning, for their behavior, or for their peers in school will probably have a difficult time accepting responsibility in the work force and in later life.

The following chapters depict scenarios in which students have trouble accepting their responsibility as group members. The scenarios show how irresponsible behavior on the part of one or two students can make groups dysfunctional. At the end of each scenario teachers are asked to brainstorm additional tactics that can be used to help the students and the group.

Students Who Are Frequently Absent

"Where's Johnny?"

Mrs. Brown signals her students to be quiet and focus their attention on her as she describes the day's activities.

"Today, we will divide our thirty vocabulary words into three groups and teach each other ten words by writing them and drawing a picture of them. After you jigsaw the words, you are responsible for teaching them to each member of the group."

"Any questions? Okay, now move into your groups. You have thirty minutes to draw and teach the words."

"Oh great," mutters Jane to Sue. *"Patrick is absent again. That's the third day this week."*

"Yeah," replies Sue. *"I'm tired of doing extra work to pick up his slack. He just doesn't like coming to school. Let's talk to Mrs. Brown about changing our base group. If she won't, I am going to get my mom and dad to come up here. It's just not fair!"*

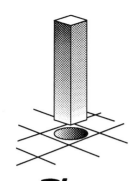

The Challenge

STUDENTS WHO ARE FREQUENTLY ABSENT

Many teachers have experienced the frustration of working with students who are chronically absent from class. Students develop their attendance patterns as early as kindergarten. Generally speaking, a senior in high school who is frequently absent was probably also frequently absent as a first grader.

In the traditional classroom, the teacher is the one who must spend time helping absentee students understand all the material they missed, keep up with their work, and make up all assignments and tests. The students, the teacher, and perhaps the parents are involved in the process, but the other students in the class are usually not involved.

In the cooperative classroom, however, the other students in the cooperative group are also affected. John Donne's famous line about "No man is an island, entire of itself" is applicable to the cooperative group. If one member is absent and doesn't pull his or her weight, everyone suffers. When a group member does not fulfill his or her obligation, "the bell tolls" for everyone in the group. Moreover, the cohesiveness of the group can break down and the other students begin to get resentful and frustrated because of their member's apparent lack of interest.

The teacher's first priority is to determine the real cause of a student's chronic absenteeism. Is the student prone to illness? Does he have a serious medical problem? Is she bored with school? Do his parents need him to babysit or work? The following strategy could be used to ascertain the root of the problem.

FOCUS STRATEGY:

Problem-Solving Model

The student should meet with the teacher and fill out the following problem-solving sheet to try to discover the cause of the problem and a mutual plan of action.

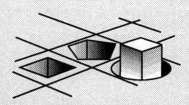

Strategy

Student: _Patrick Absentee_   Date: _Friday, April 18_

Teacher: _Mrs. Brown_

Student's Statement of the Problem:
I often have a stomach ache when I get up in the morning. My mom lets me stay home while she goes
to work.

Teacher's Statement of the Problem:
I am having a difficult time assigning you to a group because everyone knows you will be absent a lot
and they'll have to do more work.

Student's Solutions to the Problem:
1. _Don't assign me to a group; let me work alone._
2. _Put me in a larger group so they will have extra people to do work._
3. _If I feel sick, I will try to come to school anyway and then call my mom later if I need to check out_
   and go home.
4. _Have someone call me with the assignment._
5. _Move me around a lot so I won't always be in the same group._

Rank Order Three Solutions:
1. _Put me in a larger group._
2. _Have someone call me with the assignment._
3. _I will try to come to school and then call my mom to pick me up if I get sick._

Discuss Why Solution Number One is the Best Choice:
If you put me in a larger group, they won't be mad at me if I am not there as much.

Plan of Action:
We are going to put Patrick in a larger group and assign one person in the group to call him each
night he is absent to give him the assignment so he can help the group when he returns and not get
behind in his grades.

FOCUS STRATEGY continued

Time line:
April 21 to Friday April 25

Next Meeting: _Monday, April 28_

Signature of Student: _Patrick Absentee_

Signature of Teacher: _Mrs. Brown_

Signature of Parent: _Mrs. Absentee_

Phone conference with Parent: _Friday, April 18_
I talked with Patrick's mom, and she said she was aware of our agreement. She also said she
would encourage Patrick to come to school more often, and she would agree to pick him up during
the day if he got sick.

OTHER POSSIBLE STRATEGIES TO USE

❑ Review the absentee patterns of all students before assigning base groups. **Put an extra person in the groups that have a student who is frequently absent.**

❑ **Talk privately to the student** who is frequently absent to find out if personal or family problems are causing the absences.

❑ **Initiate a one-on-one conference with the absentee student** to find out if he or she feels inadequate because of a learning disability, low-ability skills, or lack of understanding of the material.

❑ **Interview the student** to find out if there is a personality conflict with one or more group members.

❑ **Organize a make-up work system** where absentee students are responsible for doing the same amount and caliber of work as the other group members.

Now Add Some of Your Own Strategies for Handling the Type of Problem Described in the Scenario

❑ _____
_____
_____

❑ _____
_____
_____

❑ _____
_____
_____

❑ _____
_____
_____

❑ _____
_____
_____

❑ _____
_____
_____

❑ _____
_____
_____

❑ _____
_____
_____

❑ _____
_____
_____

❑ _____
_____
_____

❑ _____
_____
_____

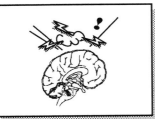

YOUR BRAINSTORMS ...

Use the scenario at the beginning of this chapter or a similar problem scenario you have encountered to solve this problem and develop an action plan.

1 **Possible Quick-Recovery Solutions to the Problem**

_____
_____
_____

2 **Possible Next-Step Solutions**

_____
_____
_____

3 **Possible Long-Term Solutions**

_____
_____
_____

Rank Order the Solutions Within Each Classification

1 "QUICK RECOVERY"

1._____
_____
_____
2._____
_____
_____
3._____
_____
_____

2 "NEXT STEP"

1._____
_____
_____
2._____
_____
_____
3._____
_____
_____

3 "LONG TERM"

1._____
_____
_____
2._____
_____
_____
3._____
_____
_____

SKYLIGHT PUBLISHING, INC.

Explain *why* you ranked each solution first.

1 **Quick-Recovery Solution**

_____

_____

_____

2 **Next-Step Solution**

_____

_____

_____

3 **Long-Term Solution**

_____

_____

_____

Sequence the steps you will take to help solve this problem.

Step 1	Step 2	Step 3

Step 4	Step 5	Step 6

Assess the effectiveness of your action plan:

_____

_____

_____

_____

_____

How will you celebrate your success?:

_____

_____

_____

_____

Reflect on a similar behavior problem you have had, review how you handled the problem at the time, and speculate about what you would do differently if you encounter the same problem again.

Problem:

_____

_____

_____

_____

What you did:

_____

_____

_____

_____

What you would do in the future:

_____

_____

_____

_____

Students Who Forget to Bring Their Work

The students are excited about their presentations in Mr. Smith's social studies class. Each group is responsible for preparing a thirty-minute presentation covering a decade in the twentieth century.

Yesterday's group presented a lesson on the 1920s. They all dressed up in flapper dresses

"The dog ate it!"

and long fur coats and skimmer hats. They also played Charleston music in the background as they showed slides of famous people and events from the '20s. Bob's group is set to present today.

"Hey, Juan," cries Bob. *"Do you have the Depression costumes ready?"*

"Sure," replies Juan, *"I'll go to my locker to get them."*

"Where's Ellen with our '30s albums? We need the background music to get the feel of the Depression."

Ellen runs into the room visibly upset. *"You guys, I called home but nobody's there!"*

"What do you mean?" asks Juan.

"I left the albums on the kitchen table, and my mom's at work and the office won't let me check out to go home and get the albums. Do you think Mr. Smith will let us do our presentation tomorrow? It won't be the same without the music."

"I don't know," says Bob. *"He assigned one presentation per day until the end of the quarter. I don't know when we'd have a chance to do it again."*

"Yeah," snarls Juan. *"We might as well do it today and just get a lower grade for not being prepared. It's better than getting a zero."*

"Thanks a lot, Ellen. This assignment is thirty percent of our total grade. You just blew it for all of us."

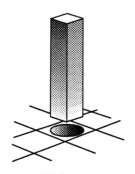

The Challenge

STUDENTS WHO FORGET TO BRING THEIR WORK

All students forget things, but some students tend to forget things on a regular basis. They often grow up to be adults who forget things on a regular basis. In a traditional classroom, students who forget their homework or something necessary for class are usually penalized by losing points, getting a detention, or receiving a zero. When a student's forgetfulness penalizes the entire group, however, the teacher must develop guidelines to handle the situation as equitably as possible. Often this type of scenario poses tremendous problems for the teacher who is trying to instill responsibility in students, but doesn't want to destroy the delicate "bonding" structure of a group by making the guiltless group members suffer for the failings of one student.

The teacher can suggest a series of organizational tips to help the student who consistently forgets. Students can learn to use a "To Do" list by writing down all the things they have to do in a daytimer, pad, or notebook. They can also put post-it notes inside their locker door, their bedroom door, or their car dashboard to remind them of important things. Or, they can keep a weekly or monthly calendar with an assignment sheet for all of their classes.

FOCUS STRATEGY:
Assignment & Test Sheet

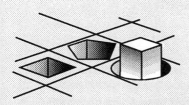

Distribute this sheet to all students in the class or specific students who have problems with organizational skills. Check to make sure they are keeping up with their work.

Strategy

Assignments	Course	Due Date	Done
1. Problems at end of Ch. 23	Math	May 17	✓
2. Abstract on article	Science	May 19	✓
3. Bring albums for skit	English	May 16	
4. Read <u>Profiles in Courage</u>	Social Studies	May 24	
5. Complete chalk drawing	Art	May 25	
6.			
7.			
8.			
9.			
10.			
11.			

Tests and Quizzes	Course	Date	Grade
1. Equations	Math	May 15	87%
2. Hormones	Science	May 18	92%
3. Depression of 1930s	English	May 23	81%
4. <u>Profiles in Courage</u>	Social Studies	May 26	95%
5.			
6.			
7.			
8.			
9.			

OTHER POSSIBLE STRATEGIES TO USE

❑ If at all possible, **allow group to present the next day.**

❑ **Talk to the group** and find out the whole story before making a decision.

❑ **Do not penalize the group** members by lowering their grades.

❑ **Talk to the student** who did not do his share to determine how his grade will be affected (minus points, late grade, lower grade, chance for extra credit, etc.).

❑ **Persuade the group members to refrain from taking out their frustration on the delinquent group member.** This might preserve the "bonding" that has taken place within the group.

❑ **Talk privately with the student** who forgot her work to find out if any personal or family problems are involved.

❑ **Talk privately with the student** to make sure he is aware of how the other group members feel and to let him know that other groups will not want him as a group member if he continues to forget his work.

❑ **Remind the student that her grade will be affected** by her inability to meet deadlines or to complete her work in a timely manner.

Now Add Some of Your Own Solutions for Handling the Problem Described in the Scenario

❑ _____
_____
_____

❑ _____
_____
_____

❑ _____
_____
_____

❑ _____
_____
_____

❑ _____
_____
_____

❑ _____
_____
_____

❑ _____
_____
_____

❑ _____
_____
_____

❑ _____
_____
_____

❑ _____
_____
_____

❑ _____
_____
_____

❑ _____
_____
_____

❑ _____
_____
_____

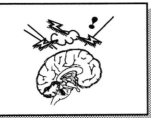

YOUR BRAINSTORMS …

Use the scenario at the beginning of this chapter or a similar problem scenario you have encountered to solve this problem and develop an action plan.

1 **Possible Quick-Recovery Solutions to the Problem**

_____

_____

_____

2 **Possible Next-Step Solutions**

_____

_____

_____

3 **Possible Long-Term Solutions**

_____

_____

_____

Rank Order the Solutions Within Each Classification

1	**2**	**3**
"QUICK RECOVERY"	**"NEXT STEP"**	**"LONG TERM"**
1._____	1._____	1._____
_____	_____	_____
_____	_____	_____
2._____	2._____	2._____
_____	_____	_____
_____	_____	_____
3._____	3._____	3._____
_____	_____	_____
_____	_____	_____

SKYLIGHT PUBLISHING, INC.

Explain *why* you ranked each solution first.

1 **Quick-Recovery Solution**

_____

_____

_____

2 **Next-Step Solution**

_____

_____

_____

3 **Long-Term Solution**

_____

_____

_____

Sequence the steps you will take to help solve this problem.

Step 1	Step 2	Step 3

Step 4	Step 5	Step 6

SKYLIGHT PUBLISHING, INC.

Assess the effectiveness of your action plan:

_____

_____

_____

_____

_____

How will you celebrate your success?:

_____

_____

_____

_____

Reflect on a similar behavior problem you have had, review how you handled the problem at the time, and speculate about what you would do differently if you encounter the same problem again.

Problem:

_____

_____

_____

_____

What you did:

_____

_____

_____

_____

What you would do in the future:

_____

_____

_____

_____

Students Who Will Not
Accept Their Roles

"I hate being the recorder!"

Mr. James asks his seventh graders to go out in the hall quietly and line up in order of the day and month of their birthdays. He tells them, *"Line up from the front of the hall to the back without saying a word. You may communicate non-verbally!"*

The eager students soon figure out how to use their fingers to hold up their birth months and days and get in line in the correct order.

After all the students line up in order, they call out their birthdays to see whether or not they have lined up correctly. Mr. James then separates the groups into threes and designates the group roles.

"The student in each group of three with the earliest birthday will be the recorder. The student with the middle birthday will be the organizer, and the student with the latest birthday will be the materials manager. Okay, you all have your roles. Now let's get started on today's cooperative group activity that I introduced earlier."

"Yuk," mutters Janis. *"I don't like being the recorder. I'm no secretary. I'd rather be the materials manager. They don't do anything."*

"No way," replies Harry. *"We all got our roles. It's your turn to record. Now quit complaining and start writing. I'm the organizer and I say get to work!"*

Janis refuses to pick up the marker when Sal, the materials manager, hands it to her.

"No," says Janis. *"I'm going to sit this one out in the 'time-out' corner."*

As she throws down her book and heads toward a desk in the corner of the room, both Harry and Sal have their hands raised to get the attention of the teacher.

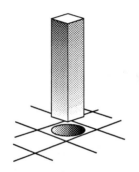

The Challenge

STUDENTS WHO WILL NOT ACCEPT THEIR ROLES

Many teachers have encountered students like Janis who do not want to do the role they were assigned. The teacher is tempted just to change the role rather than endure a confrontation with a petulant student. After all, "Mary is in Janis' group and Mary has beautiful handwriting. She would love to be the recorder." The reality, however, is that rotating the roles is an essential component of the cooperative group process. Students must learn how to lead, how to follow, how to write, how to read, how to report, and how to do a number of other life skills. After all, if teachers did not assign and rotate the roles in cooperative groups, the group members would revert to traditional work groups and allow the dominant student to lead, the student with good penmanship to write, the artistic student to draw, and the verbal student to speak. Students would then only reinforce skills they have already mastered. They would not, however, receive the opportunity to learn new skills and apply them to the overall group effort.

It is imperative, therefore, that teachers continually rotate the roles in cooperative groups. When a student refuses to accept a role, the teacher must explore the problem by trying to ascertain or sense the "real problem." The following Problem-Solving Model represents one way for the teacher to process the situation and come up with a course of action.

FOCUS STRATEGY:
Problem-Solving Model

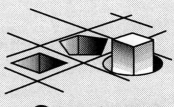

Strategy

Teacher and student should fill out this sheet together in order to arrive at possible solutions.

Student: _Janis Recordo_   Problem: _Does not want to accept her role as recorder._

Teacher: _Mr. James_   Date: _Nov. 7_

Describe the Incident:
Janis prefers to go to the "time-out" area and do the work on her own rather than accept her group role and remain a contributing member of the group.

Probe for Causes of Behavior:
Janis says she feels inadequate about her writing skills. She does not spell well and her grammar is weak. She says she is embarrassed to write things because her group members will laugh.

Brainstorm Possible Solutions to the Problem:
1. _Pair Janis with a sensitive partner who could help tutor her in grammar and spelling skills._
2. _Give Janis extra help after school in writing skills._
3. _Assign the role of "Grammar Guru" to each group. Let a student who has good grammar skills serve as an "advisor" for the group._
4. _Give a dictionary to each group and assign somebody the role of "Spell Checker" to proofread all written materials._
5. _Reinforce social skills of encouragement and support so team members help each other rather than criticize or make fun of each other._

List Top Three Solutions:
1. _Reinforce social skills for all groups._
2. _Pair Janis with sensitive student._
3. _Tutor her after school in writing skills._

Establish Time Line: Date:
1. _Reinforce social skills._   _Nov. 10_
2. _Pair Janis with sensitive student._   _Nov. 13_
3. _Tutor her after school._   _Each Tuesday_

Follow-up Meeting: _Nov. 21_
Teacher's Signature: _Mr. James_   Student's Signature: _Janis Recordo_

SKYLIGHT PUBLISHING, INC.

OTHER POSSIBLE STRATEGIES TO USE

❏ **Remind the entire class** of the social skills discussed and reviewed at the beginning of the year.

❏ **Talk with the student privately** to find out if the student feels inadequate for the role. For example, one student may not want to be the recorder because he does not write or spell very well. Another student may not want to present the material because she is afraid to talk in front of a group.

❏ **Remind the student** that all the roles rotate in group work and that if he does not like this role, he will only have to do it for a short while before the roles rotate in the next group activity.

❏ **Allow the student to go to a 'time-out' area** and either let her return when she is ready to fulfill her role or have her stay out until the entire activity is completed. (It's a right to work alone, a privilege to work in a group.)

❏ If the student elects to stay in the 'time-out' area for the entire activity, **make sure he is held accountable** for the whole activity.

❏ **Try placing role cards** with the picture or title of the role on one side and specific tasks for the role on the other side on the desks to help students understand their roles.

Now Add Some of Your Own Solutions for Handling the Problem Described in the Scenario

❏ _____
_____
_____

❏ _____
_____
_____

❏ _____
_____
_____

❑ _____
   _____
   _____

❑ _____
   _____
   _____

❑ _____
   _____
   _____

❑ _____
   _____
   _____

❑ _____
   _____
   _____

❑ _____
   _____
   _____

❑ _____
   _____
   _____

❑ _____
   _____
   _____

❑ _____
   _____
   _____

❑ _____
   _____
   _____

❑ _____
   _____
   _____

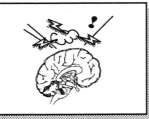

YOUR BRAINSTORMS …

Use the scenario at the beginning of this chapter or a similar problem scenario you have encountered to solve this problem and develop an action plan.

1 **Possible Quick-Recovery Solutions to the Problem**

_____

_____

_____

2 **Possible Next-Step Solutions**

_____

_____

_____

3 **Possible Long-Term Solutions**

_____

_____

_____

Rank Order the Solutions Within Each Classification

1	**2**	**3**
"QUICK RECOVERY"	**"NEXT STEP"**	**"LONG TERM"**
1._____	1._____	1._____
_____	_____	_____
_____	_____	_____
2._____	2._____	2._____
_____	_____	_____
_____	_____	_____
3._____	3._____	3._____
_____	_____	_____
_____	_____	_____

Explain *why* you ranked each solution first.

1 **Quick-Recovery Solution**

_____

_____

_____

2 **Next-Step Solution**

_____

_____

_____

3 **Long-Term Solution**

_____

_____

_____

Sequence the steps you will take to help solve this problem.

Step 1

Step 2

Step 3

Step 4

Step 5

Step 6

SKYLIGHT
PUBLISHING, INC.

Assess the effectiveness of your action plan:

_____

_____

_____

_____

_____

How will you celebrate your success?:

_____

_____

_____

_____

Reflect on a similar behavior problem you have had, review how you handled the problem at the time, and speculate about what you would do differently if you encounter the same problem again.

Problem:

_____

_____

_____

_____

What you did:

_____

_____

_____

_____

What you would do in the future:

_____

_____

_____

_____

11

Students Who Are Off Task

"*Today, students, we will start our unit on dinosaurs. How many of you know something about dinosaurs?"*

"*Good, I see that many of you have your hands raised,*" says Ms. Jones. "*We are going to find out just how much you do know by doing something called a K-W-L.*"

"How about those Bears!"

"*When I give you the signal, I want you to get into your groups and brainstorm all the things you THINK you know about dinosaurs in the left-hand column of your chart under 'K.' You already have your role assignments, so timekeepers remind your group members when ten minutes is up. You may begin!"*

The students quietly form their groups and begin brainstorming what they know about dinosaurs. Timmy, however, starts drawing his favorite football player while the other group members work on their K-W-L.

"*Timmy,*" Ann calls. "*You are the organizer this time. Put away your picture and help us with this. We'll never finish in ten minutes.*"

Timmy shrugs his shoulders and continues to draw, oblivious to the other group members and the K-W-L. Frustrated, Ann and Mary Jo start brainstorming on their own. Pretty soon, Ms. Jones comes up to the group and asks how many ideas they have brainstormed.

"Only five," cries Ann. *"Timmy isn't helping us."*

"Make him help us, Ms. Jones. We always end up doing his share. Everybody else always gets better grades and finishes before us. Put him in another group."

Timmy smiles sweetly and continues coloring in the player's helmet.

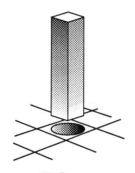

The Challenge

STUDENTS WHO ARE OFF TASK

Students have always been off task in school. Most teachers have observed students doodling, writing notes to their boyfriends or girlfriends, staring out the window, working on crossword puzzles, or sleeping. Off-task behavior is not new, but it can become more noticeable and more frustrating when it is experienced in a cooperative group setting.

In the above scenario, the other group members do not tolerate Timmy's love for football at the expense of their dinosaur assignment. Their low tolerance may turn to anger and more serious behavior problems if Timmy's off-task behavior is not addressed and corrected.

The Decision-Making Model is one method that could be used to help Timmy make his own decision about staying in the group and doing his work, going to the time-out area and doing the work on his own, or receiving a zero for his part and also alienating other group members. In the process of filling out this chart, the student carefully analyzes decisions about his behavior and the possible consequences of his decision.

FOCUS STRATEGY:
Decision-Making Model

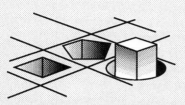

Have the student fill in the top line "What is the dilemma?" Help the student brainstorm alternatives, consequences, and pros and cons of each choice before he arrives at his decision.

Strategy

Start
⬇

WHAT IS THE DILEMMA?

> *Will I work on the K-W-L on dinosaurs with my group?*

ALTERNATIVES

I can work with my group.	*I can keep drawing and ignore the group assignment.*	*I can go to time out area and do it on my own.*	*I can refuse to participate.*

CONSEQUENCES

My group will like me – I'll get a good grade. +	*I'll make a drawing I can be proud of.* +	*I can finish my drawings and do the K-W-L when I feel like it.* +	*I won't have to work with my group.* +
– *I won't be able to draw my football players.*	– *My group will be upset with me.*	– *It will be harder to do the K-W-L on my own.*	– *My mother will kill me.*

DECISION

> *I will help my group finish the K-W-L on dinosaurs, but I'll ask if I could draw a dinosaur for our presentation.*

Student: *Timmy Gridiron*   Teacher: *Ms. Jones*   Date: *Sept. 1*

Problem: *I don't want to do the group work. I want to draw!*

Final Decision: *I will do the K-W-L as long as my group will also let me draw a dinosaur for our presentation and they will quit bugging me.*

Follow-up meeting: *Sept. 17*

Student: *Timmy*   Teacher: *Ms. Jones*

 SKYLIGHT PUBLISHING, INC.

OTHER POSSIBLE STRATEGIES TO USE

❏ **Walk over to the student** who is off task and stand there quietly (proximity).

❏ **Quietly lean over** and ask the off-task student what he is "supposed to be doing."

❏ **Review the responsibilities** of the role the off-task student was assigned to make sure she understands what is expected of her.

❏ **Talk privately with the student** to see if there is a personal problem that is preventing him from accepting his responsibility.

❏ **Talk privately with the student** to see if he is upset with one or more group members about something.

❏ **Call the parents** of a student who is constantly off task to see if there is some explanation for this behavior.

❏ **Check with the school counselor, administrator, or special education teacher** to have the student tested for learning or behavior disabilities.

❏ **Allow five minutes of free time at the end of each activity** for students to socialize, draw, or read.

Now Add Some of Your Own Solutions for Handling the Problem Described in the Scenario

❏ _____
_____
_____

❏ _____
_____
_____

❏ _____
_____
_____

❑ _____
_____
_____
_____

❑ _____
_____
_____
_____

❑ _____
_____
_____
_____

❑ _____
_____
_____
_____

❑ _____
_____
_____
_____

❑ _____
_____
_____
_____

❑ _____
_____
_____
_____

❑ _____
_____
_____
_____

❑ _____
_____
_____
_____

❑ _____
_____
_____
_____

❑ _____
_____
_____

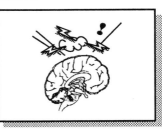

YOUR BRAINSTORMS ...

Use the scenario at the beginning of this chapter or a similar problem scenario you have encountered to solve this problem and develop an action plan.

1 **Possible Quick-Recovery Solutions to the Problem**

_____

_____

_____

2 **Possible Next-Step Solutions**

_____

_____

_____

3 **Possible Long-Term Solutions**

_____

_____

_____

Rank Order the Solutions Within Each Classification

1	**2**	**3**
"QUICK RECOVERY"	**"NEXT STEP"**	**"LONG TERM"**
1._____	1._____	1._____
2._____	2._____	2._____
3._____	3._____	3._____

Explain *why* you ranked each solution first.

1 **Quick-Recovery Solution**

_____
_____
_____

2 **Next-Step Solution**

_____
_____
_____

3 **Long-Term Solution**

_____
_____
_____

Sequence the steps you will take to help solve this problem.

| Step 1 | Step 2 | Step 3 |
| Step 4 | Step 5 | Step 6 |

Assess the effectiveness of your action plan:

_____

_____

_____

_____

_____

How will you celebrate your success?:

_____

_____

_____

_____

Reflect on a similar behavior problem you have had, review how you handled the problem at the time, and speculate about what you would do differently if you encounter the same problem again.

Problem:

_____

_____

_____

_____

What you did:

_____

_____

_____

_____

What you would do in the future:

_____

_____

_____

_____

SKYLIGHT PUBLISHING, INC.

12

Students Who Do Not Contribute

"You're not doing your share!"

"The students in Ms. Swartz's American literature course move into their base groups to continue working on their research papers on major literary figures of the twentieth century. Each group has been assigned an author's life to research together. Each member is responsible for writing his or her own paper showing how aspects of the author's life are reflected in one of his or her novels.

Nancy, Doug, and Jeff move their desks together and get out their note cards, notebooks, and the research books they are using.

"Okay, group," Nancy says: *"I have twenty note cards on Gertrude Stein's early life. Doug, what do you have about her years in France?"*

"I have lots of information about the people she hung around with," says Doug. *"I've got great quotes Stein said about Hemingway and F. Scott Fitzgerald."*

"Great, Doug. We should be ready to start our individual papers soon. What do you have about Stein's life with Alice B. Toklas, Jeff?"

"Nothing," Jeff shrugs. *"I had to work last night so I didn't get a chance to go to the library. I'll try to go this weekend when I'm off work."*

"This weekend," shrieks Nancy. *"Our paper is due next week. We can't wait until Monday to get your information. We'll never finish our own papers in time. You know that Ms. Swartz will lower our grades one letter grade if our papers are late."*

"Thanks a lot," mumbles Doug. *"We'll just have to do the research ourselves. I'm not going to let you ruin my grade in here. What a loser!"*

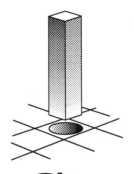

The Challenge

STUDENTS WHO DO NOT CONTRIBUTE

One of the major criticisms of cooperative learning is that some students do all of the work while others just "ride their coattails." What adult has not been a victim of a group project, a community fundraiser, a school project, or an office proposal where someone came late, left early, and did nothing! That same person often received the same grade, same reward, or same salary increase or promotion that the others did. Sadly, sometimes the one who did the least received more than everyone else. Needless to say, students in cooperative groups experience the same negative feelings when they see that one of their members is not carrying his or her weight.

First, the teacher must talk with the student who is not contributing and find out whether the problem is laziness, apathy, inadequacy, or something much deeper that must be identified if the student is to become a functional group member and a respected team player. Then, after the teacher and the student have identified the causes, the teacher may want to implement a strategy to "rebond" the group. One possible solution is to have the student write a telegram to the group explaining the problem and telling how he or she plans to correct the problem.

FOCUS STRATEGY:
Telegram

Distribute a copy of the Telegram Form to the student who is not contributing to the group. Have him address the telegram to his fellow team members and tell them how he plans to contribute to the group in the future.

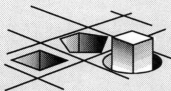

Strategy

TELEGRAM

Dateline: *January 16, Chicago, Illinois*

To: *Nancy and Doug*

From: *Jeff Procrastinator*

I am sorry I didn't have my information on Gertrude Stein ready to give you today in class. Stop
I have called my boss, and he said if I can get someone to work for me the rest of the week, I can take off. Stop
I will go to the library the next two nights and have my information to you by Friday so you can have it over the weekend. Stop
I will try to get my work done earlier. I also will try to plan my school schedule around my work schedule. I will try to do my fair share. Stop

---

OTHER POSSIBLE STRATEGIES TO USE

❑ **Give major group assignments several weeks before due dates** so students can delegate tasks and have plenty of time to finish them.

❑ **Discuss effective study skills and time management strategies** with entire class.

❑ **Use the swiss-cheese approach.** Break down major assignments into smaller tasks and have due dates for each segment.

❑ **Monitor due dates** for each segment of a major assignment to find out which students or groups are having trouble.

❏ **Try not to structure assignments** so that one student can lower the group grade. Students resent the group member and bonding erodes in the group.

❏ **Encourage group members to discuss their individual assignments** and get help from fellow group members prior to final deadline.

❏ When processing group activities, **allow students to write their evaluation of the group work.** Monitor groups whose written evaluation indicates problems with a particular group member's work.

❏ **Give students some choice in their assignments.** Students who select topics that interest them are more likely to contribute more of their time and effort.

Now Add Some of Your Own Solutions for Handling the Problem Described in the Scenario

❏ _____
_____
_____

❏ _____
_____
_____

❏ _____
_____
_____

❏ _____
_____
_____

❏ _____
_____
_____

❏ _____
_____
_____

❏ _____
_____
_____

❑ _____
_____
_____

❑ _____
_____
_____

❑ _____
_____
_____

❑ _____
_____
_____

❑ _____
_____
_____

❑ _____
_____
_____

❑ _____
_____
_____

❑ _____
_____
_____

❑ _____
_____
_____

❑ _____
_____
_____

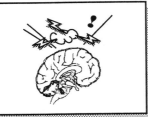

YOUR BRAINSTORMS …

Use the scenario at the beginning of this chapter or a similar problem scenario you have encountered to solve this problem and develop an action plan.

1 **Possible Quick-Recovery Solutions to the Problem**

_____
_____
_____

2 **Possible Next-Step Solutions**

_____
_____
_____

3 **Possible Long-Term Solutions**

_____
_____
_____

Rank Order the Solutions Within Each Classification

1 "QUICK RECOVERY"	**2** "NEXT STEP"	**3** "LONG TERM"
1._____	1._____	1._____
_____	_____	_____
_____	_____	_____
2._____	2._____	2._____
_____	_____	_____
_____	_____	_____
3._____	3._____	3._____
_____	_____	_____
_____	_____	_____

SKYLIGHT PUBLISHING, INC.

Explain *why* you ranked each solution first.

1 **Quick-Recovery Solution**

_____

_____

_____

2 **Next-Step Solution**

_____

_____

_____

3 **Long-Term Solution**

_____

_____

_____

Sequence the steps you will take to help solve this problem.

Step 1	Step 2	Step 3

Step 4	Step 5	Step 6

SKYLIGHT PUBLISHING, INC.

Assess the effectiveness of your action plan:

_____
_____
_____
_____
_____

How will you celebrate your success?:

_____
_____
_____
_____

Reflect on a similar behavior problem you have had, review how you handled the problem at the time, and speculate about what you would do differently if you encounter the same problem again.

Problem:

_____
_____
_____

What you did:

_____
_____
_____

What you would do in the future:

_____
_____
_____
_____

SECTION

4

STUDENTS WHO NEED HELP WITH THEIR INTERPERSONAL SKILLS

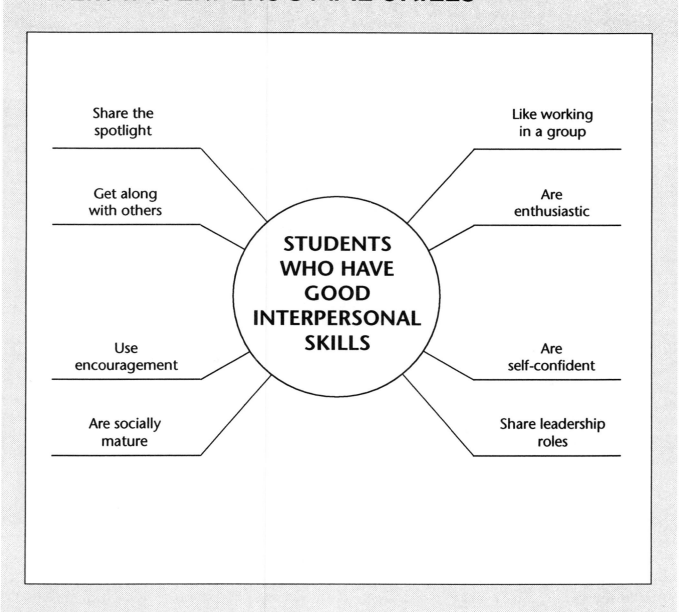

Students Who Need Help with their Interpersonal Skills

Adults who lack interpersonal skills were probably at one time students who lacked interpersonal skills. Teachers can see distinct personality problems developing in children during preschool. Too often these problems with interpersonal skills become more pronounced with each passing year. The adult who antagonizes and irritates business associates in the office was probably a first grader who bossed everyone around in the cooperative group or the one who fooled around and never did his or her share of the work. The office worker who is constantly criticizing everyone and complaining about the company was probably the student who Glasser (1986) describes as a "depressing student" who is physically inactive. "Instead of studying, participating, and doing homework, they are sitting around complaining to anyone who will listen about how much they hate school" (p. 52).

One method many teachers use to discover the individual problems that are blocking effective group interactions is the one-on-one teacher-student conference. The key to effective problem solving in a conference is reflective listening. Teachers who use "closed questions" that call for a yes-or-no answer or begin with the word "why" will tend to cut off true communication.

Sample Closed Questions

Question:	"Are you just going to sit there or are you going to get busy in your group?"
Possible Answer:	"Yes, I'm going to sit here—what are you going to do about it?"
Question:	"Do you really think your group members think you're funny?"
Possible Answer:	"Who cares!"
Question:	"Why don't you stop fooling around and get on task?"

Possible
Answer: "Because, I'm not quite finished fooling around yet."

"Closed questions" can sound accusatory, somewhat sarcastic, and negative. They antagonize students and put them on the defensive. The smart responses students sometimes give the teacher are in retaliation for the teacher embarrassing the student in front of his peers. Even if the student says nothing or replies courteously, he or she has suffered humiliation and self-esteem has been lowered. It is doubtful that "closed questions" will motivate him or her to shape up and become a stellar group member.

"Open questions," on the other hand, invite further conversation and many possible responses. They also help establish a rapport between teacher and student because they convey to the student a sense of caring and fairness.

Sample Open Questions

Question: "So, you're saying that you're upset because you don't think your group likes you. I wonder what that's all about?"

Possible
Answer: "I don't know."

Question: "Hmm. It would be interesting to know why you aren't getting along. Let's explore same possible reasons."

As the teacher listens to the student talk about the problem, he or she may want to listen for and draw out the following "subtexts."

Could it be the student would like the group to notice him more? (attention)

Could it be that other students always takes charge and she wants to be the boss? (power)

Could it be the student is upset that the group members didn't let him do the art work? (revenge)

Could it be the student feels her part of the report wouldn't be as good as the others? (inadequacy)

Dreikurs recommends that during such a discussion teachers look carefully at the student for what he calls a "recognition reflex," or an involuntary sign that the guess is correct. The reflex could be a shift in posture, a change in eye contact, or a non-verbal cue that indicates the underlying reason for the problem. Often, the student is not aware of what the real problem is and it's the teacher's job to bring it to the surface (cited in Dinkmeyer, McKay, and Dinkmeyer, 1980, p. 114).

After the initial conversation, the teacher should continue to examine the problem by arranging a private conference with the student to discuss the problem. Dinkmeyer et al. provide the following elements of an effective teacher-student conference.

1. Understand and clarify the problem.
2. Disclose the goal of the misbehavior.
3. Brainstorm alternatives (show students that what they are doing is interfering with the group process).
4. Evaluate alternative ideas.
5. Choose a solution.
6. Make a commitment to the solution and set a time and date for a follow-up conference.

(Dinkmeyer, McKay, and Dinkmeyer, 1980, p. 113-117)

Additional strategies could involve developing a social contract with students or calling in an outside neutral observer, the parents, a counselor, an administrator, or other group members.

Above all, effective conferences should be low-key, confidential, and encouraging. Both the teacher and the student should leave the conference feeling that they have been treated fairly and that they have both "won" something. Sometimes receiving the undivided attention of the teacher may encourage the student and help build his or her self-esteem.

Regardless of the strategy used, the teacher must make a concerted effort to help all those students whose poor interpersonal skills interfere with their role as productive group members. If social skills have been introduced and reinforced during the year, and if the atmosphere of the classroom is warm, caring, and non-judgmental, students should, in most cases, strive to contribute to the group process.

13

Students Who Prefer to Work by Themselves

"I vont to be alone!"

"**G**et out your art work, boys and girls. Today, you will continue working on your group projects. Put your drawings in the middle of the table and get out your supplies. Remember, everyone must work on their assigned section and contribute their fair share."

As all the group members gather around their project, Sally reaches in her book bag, pulls out a chalk sketch, and puts it on the table in front of her. She quietly begins to ink in her piece as the other two group members watch her.

"*Sally,*" Pete chides. "*We are supposed to work on one project together. Everyone else is helping their group. If you don't help us, we'll have to do more.*"

"*Yeah,*" chimes in Sandy. "*You are the best artist in our group. We need you to help us.*" Sally continues to work on her own drawing as Ms. Ryder, the art teacher, approaches the table.

"*Sally,*" Ms. Ryder says, "*Put away your drawing and help your group complete its assignment.*"

Sally looks at Ms. Ryder and says, *"I don't want to work on the group project. I want to work by myself. I'll do the same work they do and get my own grade. My mother told me I don't have to work with others if I don't want to."*

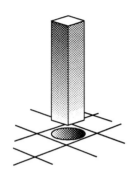

The Challenge

STUDENTS WHO PREFER TO WORK BY THEMSELVES

Some students prefer to work alone. They don't want to take the time to learn how to socialize, or they would rather do the work themselves. Jenkins (1989) describes the learning style of this type of conscientious child. The student's priority is the task or the process, and he or she loves "correctness" and "thoroughness." This type of student gains security by intense preparation and precision, and equates grades with self-worth. Conscientious children hate surprises and inaccuracy and will withdraw under tension. They want quality, privacy, accuracy, and credibility and would just as soon work alone so they have control of the final product rather than work in a group where their high standards might be compromised.

One tactic that might be successful with such students is to develop a social contract that establishes appropriate behaviors and positive consequences if they fulfill the contract obligations and negative consequences if they do not adhere to the contract. This contract would be filled out by both the student and the teacher. The "steps taken" part of the contract should be discussed in a supportive, one-on-one setting. Ideally, the student should have input into the "consequences" part of the contract also, to ensure that he or she agrees they are fair, or at least logical. Students are far more likely to adhere to the contract if they feel they have had a say in its construction.

Note that there is a spot at the end of the contract for the parent's signature. It is best if parents are given the opportunity to support and reinforce students as they strive to fulfill their part of the contract.

FOCUS STRATEGY:
Social Contract with Teacher

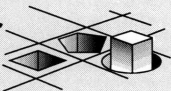

Arrange a conference with the student who prefers to work alone.
Fill out the Social Contract together and then send it home for the
parent's signature.

Strategy

Student: ___*Sally Garbo*___   Teacher: ___*Ms. Ryder*___   Date: *February 26*___

Teacher: Describe the problem.

Sally does not help her group members in Art class. She prefers to work alone on her own projects. She does an excellent job on all her individual art assignments, but her behavior in her group is anti-social and the group members do not want her in their group.

Student: What is your reaction to the problem your teacher has described?

I don't want to be in the stupid group in the first place. Pete is sloppy and can't even draw a square. Sandy spends more time putting on her lipstick than she does drawing. I enjoy art and I love doing a good job on all my projects. I know I can do better work by myself than I could do in a group of artistic mutants.

Teacher and Student: Decide on a Social Contract to help solve the problem.

Steps Taken by the Teacher:
1. *I will assign more individual projects so Sally can have more opportunities to do her own work.*
2. *I will monitor Sally's group more carefully to make sure each group member is on task.*
3. *I will rotate groups more frequently so Sally has a chance to work with other students.*
4. *I will allow Sally to do enrichment art projects on her own and allow her to share them with the whole class.*

Steps Taken by the Student:
1. *I will be more tolerant of my group members' artistic talents.*
2. *I will contribute to the group more and try to share my skills by teaching them about art.*
3. *I will try to be more friendly and cooperative with my group.*
4. *I will help my group on the big projects so we can all be proud of our work when we display it.*

Positive consequences of fulfilling the Social Contract.

1. *Sally can have a "showing" of her art work in the library.*
2. *Sally can be a "buddy" to students in the lower grades by tutoring them in art.*
3. *Sally can demonstrate an art lesson to the whole class.*

Negative consequences of **not** fulfilling the Social Contract.

1. *Sally will be penalized in her grade for not demonstrating social skills and accepting responsibility.*
2. *Sally will lose the friendship or respect of her classmates.*

FOCUS STRATEGY continued

What is the timeline for the contract?
February 26 to March 7

When and where will we meet again to discuss the results of the Social Contract?

Place: Ms. Ryder's room
Time: 3:30
Date: March 7

Student's Signature: ___*Sally Garbo*___   Date: ___*February 26*___

Teacher's Signature: ___*Ms. Ryder*___   Date: ___*February 26*___

Parent's Signature: ___*Mrs. Garbo*___   Date: ___*February 27*___

OTHER POSSIBLE STRATEGIES TO USE

❑ **Review social skills** and emphasize the importance of everyone contributing his or her fair share.

❑ **Use a jigsaw activity** where every member of the group is assigned a part of an assignment to share with the rest of the group.

❑ **Assign the reluctant worker a special assignment** that she will especially enjoy.

❑ **Assign students to groups of two for certain activities.** Make sure to pair the student who prefers to work alone with a nurturing and supportive student who will encourage him to cooperate.

❑ **Talk with the student individually** to find out if the problem is personal or group-related.

❑ **Talk to the other group members** confidentially to find out if they know why the student does not like working with the group.

❏ **Call the parents of the student** who is withdrawing from group interactions to find out if they know why she doesn't like working in a group.

Now Add Some of Your Own Solutions for Handling the Problem Described in the Scenario

❏ _____
_____
_____

❏ _____
_____
_____
_____

❏ _____
_____
_____
_____

❏ _____
_____
_____

❏ _____
_____
_____

❏ _____
_____
_____

❏ _____
_____
_____

❏ _____
_____
_____

❏ _____
_____
_____

❏ _____
_____
_____

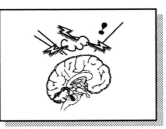

YOUR BRAINSTORMS …

Use the scenario at the beginning of this chapter or a similar problem scenario you have encountered to solve this problem and develop an action plan.

1 **Possible Quick-Recovery Solutions to the Problem**

_____
_____
_____

2 **Possible Next-Step Solutions**

_____
_____
_____

3 **Possible Long-Term Solutions**

_____
_____
_____

Rank Order the Solutions Within Each Classification

1 "QUICK RECOVERY"	**2** "NEXT STEP"	**3** "LONG TERM"
1._____ _____ _____ 2._____ _____ _____ 3._____ _____ _____	1._____ _____ _____ 2._____ _____ _____ 3._____ _____ _____	1._____ _____ _____ 2._____ _____ _____ 3._____ _____ _____

SKYLIGHT PUBLISHING, INC.

Explain *why* you ranked each solution first.

1 **Quick-Recovery Solution**

_____

_____

_____

2 **Next-Step Solution**

_____

_____

_____

3 **Long-Term Solution**

_____

_____

_____

Sequence the steps you will take to help solve this problem.

| Step 1 | Step 2 | Step 3 |

| Step 4 | Step 5 | Step 6 |

 SKYLIGHT PUBLISHING, INC.

Assess the effectiveness of your action plan:

_____

_____

_____

_____

_____

How will you celebrate your success?:

_____

_____

_____

_____

Reflect on a similar behavior problem you have had, review how you handled the problem at the time, and speculate about what you would do differently if you encounter the same problem again.

Problem:

_____

_____

_____

_____

What you did:

_____

_____

_____

_____

What you would do in the future:

_____

_____

_____

_____

14

Students Who Are Apathetic

As the students reach into the box and pull out a card, they look around for students who have the same colored dots to find their new group members.

Russ draws a double red dot so he joins Ted and Jill at a table. *"Since I'm the organizer,"* Jill announces, *"I'll assign each person their reading assignment. Russ, you read the first page."*

"I don't care what you guys do"

"No." Russ replies. *"I don't want to read."*

"You have to," says Jill. *"Everyone is supposed to read a page and I picked you to go first!"*

"No," Russ mumbles.

"Okay," Jill says. *"Let's just go on. I'll read."* Jill begins to read as Russ closes his book, crosses his arms, and stares at the clock.

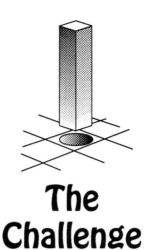

The Challenge

STUDENTS WHO ARE APATHETIC

Unfortunately, teachers tend to ignore apathetic students because they are so quiet and unobtrusive. A teacher's silence is a subtle form of discouragement. Dinkmeyer and Losoncy (1980) say that "human beings increase their self-esteem, self-confidence, and feelings of worth when they are recognized" (p. 59). If teachers and students do not provide positive feedback to an individual who feels apathetic when that person makes an effort or makes progress, the individual may feel his or her behavior is unacceptable.

Failure to recognize the student's attempt to cooperate may stop the individual's effort to improve. Lack of feedback for positive behavior can be interpreted as negative feedback. Teachers and fellow group members cannot ignore the "quiet" group members because those who perceive themselves as being inadequate will need constant reinforcement, encouragement, and positive feedback if they are to become productive group members.

Students who choose not to get involved may benefit from the Decision-Making Model. They can list what they perceive their problem to be, their goal, and the pros and cons of the alternatives they have. The self-analysis element of this model will help students explore their options and perhaps make better choices.

FOCUS STRATEGY:
Decision-Making Model

Ask the student who is apathetic to write in the problem as he or she sees it. Have the student brainstorm alternatives to the problem and then analyze the pros and cons for each solution before arriving at the final decision.

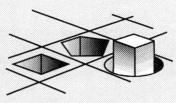

Strategy

Student: *Russ Ennui*   Date: *March 3*   Teacher: *Mrs. Moss*

Problem
   Kids don't like me because I don't do anything. No one wants me in their group.

Alternative Solutions	Pros and Cons

Solution #1
   I could work by myself in the time-out area all the time.

Pro   *The group won't bother me anymore.*

Con   *It's harder to do everything all by myself.*

Solution #2
   I could get some extra help in reading after school. I don't like to read in front of people because they might laugh.

Pro   *I wouldn't mind reading aloud if I read better.*

Con   *I'd rather watch TV than stay after school.*

Solution #3
   I could admit to the groups that I don't like to read, but I would volunteer to record or draw because I'm a good artist.

Pro   *I like to draw.*

Con   *I can't draw all the time.*

Final Decision
   I will talk to the teacher and ask her for extra help in reading after school. I will also ask not to be the reader until I'm ready.

Reasons
   If I do art work or get materials for a while, I'll feel good. Then when I feel ready – I'll be the reader.

SKYLIGHT
PUBLISHING, INC.

OTHER POSSIBLE STRATEGIES TO USE

❑ **Temporarily assign student easy roles and less challenging tasks** to build his self-esteem and self-confidence.

❑ **Talk to the parents** to find out if the student has had problems relating to people.

❑ **Ask the student what things she would like to do in the group** and see if new roles or tasks could be arranged.

❑ **Orchestrate the groups** so that the apathetic student gets into a group of students who will support, encourage, and praise him.

❑ **Encourage the student** by "catching her being good" whenever she contributes something worthwhile to the group.

❑ **Pair the student with one other** supportive student.

❑ **Discover any special talents the student has** and make sure he can display those talents in the group setting, e.g., art work, computer use, speaking, props, etc.

❑ **Give the student a lead role in the group** so she feels important and involved.

Now Add Some of Your Own Solutions for Handling the Problem Described in the Scenario

❑ _____
_____
_____

❑ _____
_____
_____

❑ _____
_____
_____

❑ _____
_____
_____

❑ _____
  _____
  _____

❑ _____
  _____
  _____

❑ _____
  _____
  _____

❑ _____
  _____
  _____

❑ _____
  _____
  _____

❑ _____
  _____
  _____

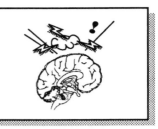

YOUR BRAINSTORMS …

Use the scenario at the beginning of this chapter or a similar problem scenario you have encountered to solve this problem and develop an action plan.

1 **Possible Quick-Recovery Solutions to the Problem**

_____

_____

_____

2 **Possible Next-Step Solutions**

_____

_____

_____

3 **Possible Long-Term Solutions**

_____

_____

_____

Rank Order the Solutions Within Each Classification

1	**2**	**3**
"QUICK RECOVERY"	**"NEXT STEP"**	**"LONG TERM"**
1._____	1._____	1._____
2._____	2._____	2._____
3._____	3._____	3._____

SKYLIGHT PUBLISHING, INC.

Explain *why* you ranked each solution first.

1 **Quick-Recovery Solution**

_____

_____

_____

2 **Next-Step Solution**

_____

_____

_____

3 **Long-Term Solution**

_____

_____

_____

Sequence the steps you will take to help solve this problem.

Step 1	**Step 2**	**Step 3**

Step 4	**Step 5**	**Step 6**

SKYLIGHT PUBLISHING, INC.

Assess the effectiveness of your action plan:

_____
_____
_____
_____
_____

How will you celebrate your success?:

_____
_____
_____
_____

Reflect on a similar behavior problem you have had, review how you handled the problem at the time, and speculate about what you would do differently if you encounter the same problem again.

Problem:

_____
_____
_____
_____

What you did:

_____
_____
_____
_____

What you would do in the future:

_____
_____
_____
_____

15

Students Who Dominate the Group

"Okay, here's how it should be done"

"I've got a great idea," shouts Mark. *"Let's do a mind map of the Middle Ages for our social studies project. We can draw pictures to represent the crusades, architecture, the bubonic plague, and feudalism. Then we can draw smaller circles to brainstorm all the things that fall under those headings."*

"Yeah, I like that idea," says Rita. *"We can get a large sheet of newsprint or some colored markers. I can cut up some pictures I found in mom's old history book and we can glue them around the mind map."*

"That's a dumb idea," interjects Rosa. *"Everyone does mind maps. They're boring! Here's what we'll do. We'll draw costumes of all the groups in the Middle Ages. I've got pictures we can trace."*

"Wait a minute," Mark interrupts. *"Who died and made you queen? You're the recorder this time. Why do we always have to do what you want? I'm sick of always giving in to your ideas!"*

"Very well," replies Rosa. *"You do what you want, but don't expect me to help with anything. Your idea is stupid and I'm not going to get a low grade because of you. Besides, you can't draw or spell. You need me!"*

"Okay," Mark says reluctantly. *"We'll do your costume idea, but I'm tired of you always getting your way. Haven't you ever heard of a democracy?"*

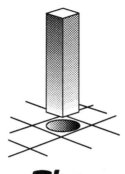

The Challenge

STUDENTS WHO DOMINATE THE GROUP

Dominant group members love being the center of attention and being in control. Jenkins (1989) describes the dominant child as having a choleric personality and as being a student who takes risks. The dominant child likes leadership, competition, and control and is irritated by indecision and inefficiency in the group. When confronted by deadlines this student will "dictate and assert."

Dominating students may offer their strength, knowledge, and organizational abilities ostensibly to "help" others, but often the real motive is to control the task because they feel the other group members won't do it as well as they can. Dominating students offer their expertise at the expense of other group members. The other group members may then lose their self-confidence and feelings of self-worth (Dinkmeyer and Losoncy, 1980).

One of the major problems with dominating students is that they often do not realize the effect their behavior has on others. A graphic organizer that might help dominating students reflect on their "bossiness" and see the effect their actions have on themselves, the teachers, and other group members is the Cause-and-Effect Model. The student might fill out this model with the teacher or with his or her group.

FOCUS STRATEGY:
Cause-and-Effect Model

Have the student who dominates the group list his or her
behaviors and the effect those behaviors have on others.

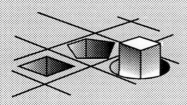

Strategy

Student: _Rosa Pushy_   Date: _October 15_   Teacher: _Mr. Williams_

Specific Behavior   Effect It Could Have on Others

I don't follow orders from other students.

My group members get upset because they never get a chance to use their ideas.

I say that my ideas are much better than some of the stupid ones they have.

I could hurt their feelings because I won't listen to them.

I don't help the group if they don't go along with my ideas.

My group members give in to my ideas but they resent doing it. I also think they resent me.

Reflection on Behaviors ___I guess I can get pretty pushy at times. I'm usually right, but I guess what___
___I say hurts people's feelings.___

Targeted Behavior to Change _I'll work on listening to others and taking turns. I think I can do it._

Signed: _Rosa Pushy_   Date: _Oct. 15_

SKYLIGHT
PUBLISHING, INC.

OTHER POSSIBLE STRATEGIES TO USE

❑ **Review social skills** of sharing, taking turns, and contributing.

❑ **Review roles** and make sure everyone is following the designated rules for each role.

❑ Give everyone in the group a different colored magic marker and **make sure each color of marker is represented on the final product.**

❑ **Talk privately with the dominating student** to determine why he or she has to be in control.

❑ **Practice five-to-fist consensus building** (see Chapter 7) with the class and groups.

❑ **Do exercises on conflict resolution** to show students how to disagree with ideas, not people.

❑ **Make the dominating student an observer** so he has to remain quiet throughout the activity.

❑ **Make the tasks more challenging** so the student has to take on more responsibility.

Now Add Some of Your Own Solutions for Handling the Problem Described in the Scenario

❑ _____
_____
_____

❑ _____
_____
_____

❑ _____
_____
_____

❑ _____
_____
_____

❑ _____
_____
_____

❑ _____
_____
_____

❑ _____
_____
_____

❑ _____
_____
_____

❑ _____
_____
_____

❑ _____
_____
_____

❑ _____
_____
_____

❑ _____
_____
_____

❑ _____
_____
_____

❑ _____
_____
_____

❑ _____
_____
_____

❑ _____
_____
_____

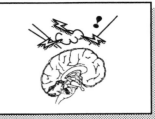

YOUR BRAINSTORMS …

Use the scenario at the beginning of this chapter or a similar problem scenario you have encountered to solve this problem and develop an action plan.

1 **Possible Quick-Recovery Solutions to the Problem**

_____

_____

_____

2 **Possible Next-Step Solutions**

_____

_____

_____

3 **Possible Long-Term Solutions**

_____

_____

_____

Rank Order the Solutions Within Each Classification

1	**2**	**3**
"QUICK RECOVERY"	"NEXT STEP"	"LONG TERM"
1._____	1._____	1._____
_____	_____	_____
_____	_____	_____
2._____	2._____	2._____
_____	_____	_____
_____	_____	_____
3._____	3._____	3._____
_____	_____	_____
_____	_____	_____

SKYLIGHT PUBLISHING, INC.

Explain *why* you ranked each solution first.

1 **Quick-Recovery Solution**

_____

_____

_____

2 **Next-Step Solution**

_____

_____

_____

3 **Long-Term Solution**

_____

_____

_____

Sequence the steps you will take to help solve this problem.

Step 1	Step 2	Step 3

Step 4	Step 5	Step 6

SKYLIGHT
PUBLISHING, INC.

Assess the effectiveness of your action plan:

_____

_____

_____

_____

_____

How will you celebrate your success?:

_____

_____

_____

_____

Reflect on a similar behavior problem you have had, review how you handled the problem at the time, and speculate about what you would do differently if you encounter the same problem again.

Problem:

_____

_____

_____

_____

What you did:

_____

_____

_____

_____

What you would do in the future:

_____

_____

_____

_____

© 1992 Skylight Publishing

SKYLIGHT
PUBLISHING, INC.

16

Students Who Do Not Get Along with Others

Mrs. Smith puts the instructions for the group activity in geometry on the overhead.

"Okay students," Mrs. Smith begins. *"When I give the signal, I would like the materials managers to pick up their bags of manipulatives so that each group can start figuring out the problems on radius and circum-*

"We don't want that kid in our group!"

ference. Remember, you have twenty minutes to solve the five problems. Work together and give each other lots of encouragement."

Mrs. Smith gives the signal and Beth, the materials manager, brings back the manipulatives to the group. Beth, Bruce, and Terry start to work the problems using their compasses and protractors. Jim, however, continues doodling on the inside corner of his geometry book.

"Earth calling Jim," Beth sings. *"Would you mind helping us?"*

"I hate math," mumbles Jim. *"I don't do geometry."*

"Aren't you going to do anything?" implores Bruce.

"Get a life," Jim laughs. *"You nerds can keep your calculators and pocket protectors, I'm out of here!"*

Jim gets up, goes to the shelf to pick up a magazine, and walks back to the "time-out" area.

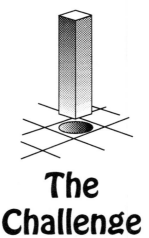

The Challenge

STUDENTS WHO DO NOT GET ALONG WITH OTHERS

Every classroom teacher has a few students who just don't get along with anybody. These students are usually socially immature, hyperactive, anti-social, obnoxious, or off-task. When these types of students are assigned to new groups, the reactions of the other group members may be:

"Oh, no! Now we'll never get anything done."

"Please, Miss Jones, we had him last time."

"Great, now we have that kid again."

"I want to go to time-out and work on my own."

"It's not fair. Now we have to do twice as much work to make up for her."

Teachers complain that a few students with weak interpersonal skills can make groups dysfunctional. And they really complain when they are assigned six or seven of these "pariahs" in one classroom. Do you put them all in the same group and hope for the best? Do you spread them out to divide and conquer? Do you not use cooperative groups because of the potential for behavior problems?

There is no "quick fix" for handling the diverse personality types that make up these categories. Underneath all the smart remarks, peer put-downs, social blunders, and bravado, however, many of these students are underachievers or students who feel inadequate and who are using their negative behavior as a smoke screen to hide their insecurities.

According to Dinkmeyer, McKay, and Dinkmeyer (1980), surveys show that approximately forty percent of all students are underachievers who perform below their abilities. Even though these underachievers often score in the top third of their class on standardized tests, they generally make poor grades and are unsuccessful in school. They tend to be impulsive and have poor interpersonal relationships. They want instant gratification and have high social goals, but their low grades cause them to have low self-esteem.

These students are frustrated by the knowledge that they are capable of doing much better. Teachers and parents expect them to do much better, but they are earning low grades and are perceived by other students as being dumb, lazy, or weird. In order to compensate for their frustration and lack of positive attention or encouragement from others, they often "act out" to attract negative attention and peer approval. Negative attention is better than no attention in their minds.

Whatever the cause of the problem, the student with poor interpersonal skills often needs guidance to change a poor relationship with group members. The following "Social Contract" is a tool the teacher can use to help the student think through the consequences of his or her behavior, and maybe improve relations with his or her group.

FOCUS STRATEGY:
Group Social Contract

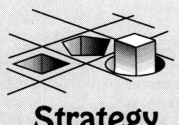

Strategy

Have the group members write down the situation from their point of view and agree on what the problem is. Have each group member write down one thing he or she would be willing to do to help solve the problem.

Group members: _Beth, Bruce, Terry, Jim_

Date: _Oct. 15_

Problem: _Jim does not like math and does not want to work in our group._

Each person's statement of what he or she can do to help solve the problem:

Jim: _I can try to be nicer to my group members. I just hate math and I don't want to do the problems. I guess I could listen more and try to learn._

Beth: _I could help Jim by reviewing his homework with him and maybe even calling him at home to see if he has questions._

Bruce: _I could quit giving Jim a bad time for not helping. I'll get off his case and give him a break._

Terry: _I could be his study buddy and review with him before quizzes and tests._

Timeline: _1 week, October 20-25_

Next meeting: _October 28, Homeroom, room 218_

Goal: _To make Jim feel part of the group and help him understand math._

How will we celebrate success: _We'll treat ourselves to ice cream at lunch the first time Jim passes a math test!_

Signed: _Terry (recorder)_   _Jim_
          Beth   _Bruce_

OTHER POSSIBLE STRATEGIES TO USE

❏ **Review social skill of encouragement versus put-downs.** Make a T-chart and have groups brainstorm what put-downs look like and sound like.

❑ **Review social skill of "doing your share"** to make sure everyone realizes the importance of contributing to the group effort.

❑ **Talk with the student one on one** to see if she feels inadequate intellectually and is masking embarrassment by acting rudely toward other group members.

❑ **Monitor the group carefully** to see if the group members are antagonizing the student who cannot get along with them.

❑ **Move the entire group closer to the front of the room** so the teacher can monitor put-downs and negative conversations.

❑ **Place the student in a pair of two students** rather than a group of three or more so he can feel more a part of the group activity. Place the student with a supportive and nurturing partner.

❑ **Rotate groups frequently.** Students may be more accepting of the student since they know they will not have to work with her too long.

❑ **Structure the group activity so that the student has a role that will ensure his success and raise self-esteem.**

❑ **Have the group write their processing of group activities in a log or journal** that only the teacher will see. Sometimes students will share their problems in writing more honestly than they will when they have to speak in front of group members.

Now Add Some of Your Own Solutions for Handling the Problem Described in the Scenario

❑ _____
_____
_____

❑ _____
_____
_____

❑ _____
_____
_____

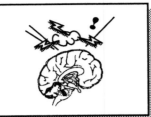

YOUR BRAINSTORMS ...

Use the scenario at the beginning of this chapter or a similar problem scenario you have encountered to solve this problem and develop an action plan.

1 **Possible Quick-Recovery Solutions to the Problem**

_____
_____
_____

2 **Possible Next-Step Solutions**

_____
_____
_____

3 **Possible Long-Term Solutions**

_____
_____
_____

Rank Order the Solutions Within Each Classification

1 "QUICK RECOVERY"	**2** "NEXT STEP"	**3** "LONG TERM"
1._____	1._____	1._____
_____	_____	_____
_____	_____	_____
2._____	2._____	2._____
_____	_____	_____
_____	_____	_____
3._____	3._____	3._____
_____	_____	_____
_____	_____	_____

SKYLIGHT PUBLISHING, INC.

Explain *why* you ranked each solution first.

1 **Quick-Recovery Solution**

_____

_____

_____

2 **Next-Step Solution**

_____

_____

_____

3 **Long-Term Solution**

_____

_____

_____

Sequence the steps you will take to help solve this problem.

Step 1	**Step 2**	**Step 3**

Step 4	**Step 5**	**Step 6**

© 1992 Skylight Publishing

Assess the effectiveness of your action plan:

_____

_____

_____

_____

_____

How will you celebrate your success?:

_____

_____

_____

_____

Reflect on a similar behavior problem you have had, review how you handled the problem at the time, and speculate about what you would do differently if you encounter the same problem again.

Problem:

_____

_____

_____

_____

What you did:

_____

_____

_____

_____

What you would do in the future:

_____

_____

_____

_____

SKYLIGHT PUBLISHING, INC.

STUDENTS WITH BEHAVIOR PROBLEMS

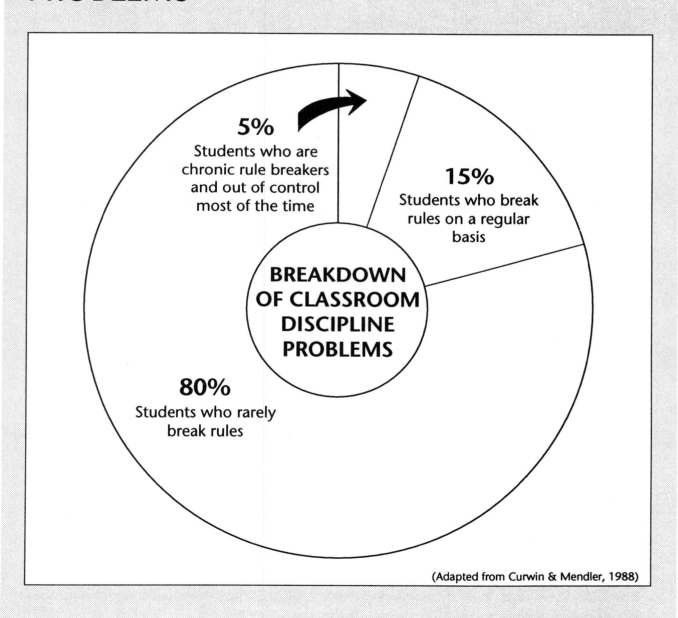

5%
Students who are chronic rule breakers and out of control most of the time

15%
Students who break rules on a regular basis

BREAKDOWN OF CLASSROOM DISCIPLINE PROBLEMS

80%
Students who rarely break rules

(Adapted from Curwin & Mendler, 1988)

Students With Behavior Problems

Despite all the latest "buzz words" of the restructuring movement, despite all the rhetoric concerning low test scores, and despite all the emphasis on higher-order thinking and lifelong learning, teachers today know that the bottom line in teaching is effective classroom management. Some of the most progressive and creative teachers have left the classroom because they could not deal with the day-to-day problems of classroom discipline. When parents discuss "what's wrong with schools," they inevitably mention discipline as the root of all the problems. Discipline has ranked as the number one problem for parents and educators for the last fifteen years (Evertson & Harris, 1992, p. 74).

Research by Walberg and Karweit indicates that the amount of time students spend learning the curriculum varies from school to school, but even under the best of circumstances, half or less of the entire school day is actually used for instruction (Evertson & Harris, 1992). Obviously, a great deal of classroom time is spent on classroom management.

Curwin and Mendler's five percent in their 80-15-5 model may be increasing. If eighty percent of the students in a class rarely break the rules and fifteen percent break rules on a regular basis, then only five percent break rules chronically. If a teacher has a class of thirty students, he or she can anticipate 1.5 chronic rule breakers on the roll. Unfortunately, most teachers today wish they had that few. The number of students with socioeconomic, alcohol, drug, and family problems is increasing. Many of these students do not find school satisfying, and they have internalized a sense of frustration and a poor self-concept from years of academic and social failures within the school system.

The hard-core discipline problems in a classroom are students who seek attention in either positive or negative ways; students who seek revenge on the teacher, other students, or their parents; students who seek power over other students, their parents and their teacher; and students who resort to aggressive behaviors.

While these types of students are disruptive and therefore easily identifiable, there are probably more students who feel inadequate than students who seek attention, power, or revenge. These students exist in great numbers, but they are often ignored. The teacher's attention is drawn to the class clown and the class bully because they are louder, and because they threaten the climate of the entire class and the leadership role of the teacher. Left alone, however, the inadequate student will quietly withdraw from class activities and may eventually drop out of school.

A teacher could spend the whole day stopping to say "Michael, stop that!" "Kathy, turn around," "Frank, put that down," and constant other "quick" ways to address the problems. Experience shows, however, that taking the time to use a long-term solution like the Newspaper Model, the Divided Journal, and the Power Struggle Graph to help analyze the problem can help by serving as a reflective piece for the student, and as a discussion vehicle for both the student and teacher.

17

Students Who Seek Attention

Glenn is new in the class. Instead of working on his chalk drawing he gets up from the group and goes over to the pencil sharpener and starts sharpening a long pencil. Each time he finishes sharpening, he puts it inside again until the pencil becomes a stub.

"I wasn't doing anything!"

"Sit down," cries John. *"We're trying to work here and you're bothering us."*

"I'm just trying to sharpen my pencil," Glenn announces loudly to the entire class. *"Is that a crime? Excuse me for living!"*

Mrs. Martinez walks over to Glenn and whispers quietly. *"Glenn your group members are working on their art project and they really need your help."*

Glenn reluctantly rejoins his group and proceeds to take a piece of hot-pink colored chalk and draw a happy face on the back of Mary's black sweater.

"You jerk," shrieks Mary. *"When are you going to grow up?"*

"What a geek," says John. *"Wouldn't you know we'd get stuck with you in our base group."*

Mrs. Martinez walks over and taps Glenn on the shoulder and they both walk into the hall.

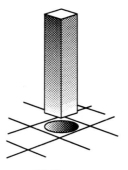

The Challenge

STUDENTS WHO SEEK ATTENTION

Experience has shown that learning problems usually precede behavior problems.... It has been found that emotional tension, aggressiveness, anxious behavior, and other disturbing symptoms seem to disappear when encouraging remedial techniques are used and the student begins to achieve in school. (Dinkmeyer, McKay, and Dinkmeyer, 1980, p. 255)

Attention seekers often do not make good cooperative group members. Attention seekers are students who seek independence, but spend a great deal of their time complaining to others that they cannot control what is happening in their lives. "They see themselves as victims of circumstance and strive to gain attention by keeping adults busy with them" (Dinkmeyer, McKay, & Dinkmeyer, 1980, p. 252).

Many attention seekers are discouraged students who may become obnoxiously loud and silly or may resort to immature acts like pushing books off a desk or trying to trip someone in order to get noticed. They do get noticed, but most of them are ultimately rejected by their peers and the teacher who grow tired of their puerile comments and childish acts. The attention seekers' idea of success is to be in the limelight, even if their actions violate the dignity and rights of other students and earn them the hostility of those who feel attacked or violated (Dinkmeyer & Losoncy, 1980).

Many students are not happy when the attention-seeking student is assigned to their group. The students are noticeably apprehensive about what "stunts" the attention seeker is planning, and they know he or she won't contribute his or her fair share. By the same token, most attention seekers are keenly aware that they are not wanted in the group and will sometimes resort to acting out to get revenge on the group.

The greatest challenge for the teacher is to change the behavior of the attention seeker by giving him or her as little attention as possible when the misbehavior is occurring. Bellanca and Fogarty (1991, p. 73) recommend the following strategies:

- Highlight other students who are behaving appropriately.
- Move the student out of the spotlight by giving him an errand to run.
- Distract the student with a task question.
- Attend to the attention seeker when he is on task.

By encouraging attention seekers to succeed in individual or group work and by noticing and praising their accomplishments, teachers and students can reinforce appropriate behavior with positive attention. The goal is to encourage attention seekers to strive for positive attention from peers rather than resort to negative attention to fulfill their needs.

One method that could be used to help attention seekers evaluate their behavior and reflect on when and why they try to get attention is the Newspaper Model graphic organizer. Sometimes a pattern emerges where it becomes evident that certain people or certain situations provoke the attention seeker to "act out." The Newspaper Model allows attention seekers to analyze their actions and reflect on the causes and effects of their behavior.

FOCUS STRATEGY:
The Newspaper Model

Ask attention seekers to state what they think the problem is. Students should then list who they think is involved, and why, where, and when the problem occurs. Finally, they should write a paragraph about the situation.

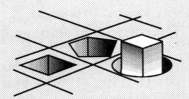

Strategy

Name: *Glenn Spotlight*   Date: *Feb. 3*

Problem: *I got in trouble for drawing on Mary's sweater but she started it.*

Who	What	When	Where	Why
Glenn	drew a happy face with colored chalk on Mary's sweater	Tuesday Feb. 3	In Mrs. Martinez' art class	Because she thinks she's hot stuff and she is always putting me down and calling me names

Write a paragraph commenting on the situation you have described above.

I got mad because John and Mary think they are better than me. They never use my ideas when we meet in groups. They are always calling me names and putting me down. I guess I shouldn't have drawn the happy face, but Mary called me a jerk and that hurt my feelings. Maybe I should apologize to her. I guess I got a little carried away.

Signed: *Glenn*

Have another group member write a paragraph about the situation.

I called Glenn a jerk because he is always fooling around instead of helping. I know I shouldn't call him names, but I get real frustrated with him.

Signed: *Mary*

OTHER POSSIBLE STRATEGIES TO USE

❑ **Do a whole group/small group lesson on friendship skills.** Discuss positive and negative ways to show friendship.

❑ **Talk to the social worker or counselor** to find out if the student has any personal or family problems that would be causing him to act out.

❑ **Help her find an area where she can shine.** Find a specific interest or strength she has so that she can get attention in a positive way.

❑ **Find the student a "study buddy."** Sometimes a student who lacks friends tries to compensate by "acting out."

❑ **Form a "New Students" cooperative group.** Have them meet during their free period or lunch time to give them a base group of other new students or a sense of security in their new surroundings.

❑ **Give the student an option of a short "time-out" period.** He can count to one hundred, reflect on his behavior, and have a chance to return to the group and improve his behavior on his own.

❑ **Increase the student's self-esteem by helping** her complete a Venn diagram of "what I do well at school" and "what I do well at home." Have her put "why I'm a good person" in the middle.

❑ **Prepare a social contract** with the student keeping track of all the times he tries to get attention. List the major things he does and review the list daily or weekly to make sure he is aware of what he does and when he does it.

❑ When a student does do something well, **praise him.**

❑ When a student raises her hand, **call on her quickly.**

❑ **Make the student the recorder** so he has to stay busy and quiet.

❑ **Give the student legitimate positive attention** by allowing her to run errands, lead the pledge, clean the board, collect papers, or other positions of responsibility and honor.

❑ **Have a secret signal** to give the student from across the room to remind her when she is doing something to get attention.

Now Add Some of Your Own Solutions for Handling the Problem Described in the Scenario

❑ _____
_____
_____

❑ _____
_____
_____

❑ _____
_____
_____

❑ _____
_____
_____

❑ _____
_____
_____

❑ _____
_____
_____

❑ _____
_____
_____

❑ _____
_____
_____

❑ _____
_____
_____

❑ _____
_____
_____

❑ _____
_____
_____

❏ _____
_____
_____
_____

❏ _____
_____
_____
_____

❏ _____
_____
_____
_____

❏ _____
_____
_____
_____

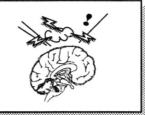

YOUR BRAINSTORMS …

Use the scenario at the beginning of this chapter or a similar problem scenario you have encountered to solve this problem and develop an action plan.

1 **Possible Quick-Recovery Solutions to the Problem**

_____

_____

_____

2 **Possible Next-Step Solutions**

_____

_____

_____

3 **Possible Long-Term Solutions**

_____

_____

_____

Rank Order the Solutions Within Each Classification

1	**2**	**3**
"QUICK RECOVERY"	**"NEXT STEP"**	**"LONG TERM"**
1._____	1._____	1._____
_____	_____	_____
_____	_____	_____
2._____	2._____	2._____
_____	_____	_____
_____	_____	_____
3._____	3._____	3._____
_____	_____	_____
_____	_____	_____

Explain *why* you ranked each solution first.

1 **Quick-Recovery Solution**

_____

_____

_____

2 **Next-Step Solution**

_____

_____

_____

3 **Long-Term Solution**

_____

_____

_____

Sequence the steps you will take to help solve this problem.

Step 1

Step 2

Step 3

Step 4

Step 5

Step 6

Assess the effectiveness of your action plan:

_____
_____
_____
_____
_____

How will you celebrate your success?:

_____
_____
_____
_____

Reflect on a similar behavior problem you have had, review how you handled the problem at the time, and speculate about what you would do differently if you encounter the same problem again.

Problem:

_____
_____
_____
_____

What you did:

_____
_____
_____
_____

What you would do in the future:

_____
_____
_____
_____

 SKYLIGHT
PUBLISHING, INC.

18

Students Who Seek Power

"No way," shouts Kim. "I'm not going to work with those eggheads again. Put me into another group or I'm out of here!"

"Kim," Mr. Love says softly as he walks quickly across the room and stands beside her. "You know our group rules. We discussed them at the beginning of the year. Sometimes we don't want to work with certain people, but we do our best to get along. Remember, you'll only be working together for a few days. You can handle that, can't you?"

"No way! I hate Mary Ellen and the rest of them. No way that _____ is going to boss me around. Either I get a new group now, or I'll go to time-out until June!"

Mary Ellen turns her back, crosses her arms, and taps her foot excitedly as she waits for Mr. Love's response.

"You can't make me do this boring stuff"

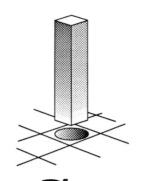

The Challenge

STUDENTS WHO SEEK POWER

I believe that the need for power is the core—the absolute core—of almost all school problems. (Glasser as cited in Gough 1987, p. 658)

Students who seek independence sometimes engage in power conflicts with adults because the students are determined not to do what adults want. Curwin and Mendler (1988) warn teachers not to get caught in a power trap: "Commit yourself to avoiding power struggles, even if it means initially backing down. Remember that continuation of a power struggle makes you look foolish and out of control. You must be prepared to see long-term victory (a cooperative, positive classroom climate) as more important than short-term winning" (p. 105).

Glasser (1986) feels that students, even good students, don't feel important in school because no one listens to them. Moreover, students who receive poor grades and are considered "discipline problems" cannot feel important from the standpoint of academic performance and acceptance. Glasser asserts that students would work harder in school if they had more freedom and fun. Cooperative activities can promote the freedom of choice and site-based decision making by the group members. Moreover, motivating and creative cooperative learning lessons can be fun as well as educational. Students need to feel that they are part of the process, not just the final products.

Most often, the power base is tilted in favor of the teachers. Teachers have the power to threaten students and back up those threats with minus points, time-out area, detention, notes to parents, suspensions, and the big one—failure. Despite all this power, Glasser says that half the students still won't work because they don't feel they have any control over their lives. They are frustrated that they have so little say about what they learn, when they learn it, and how they learn it. Students are frustrated and they don't have the patience to wait until teachers and the school system give them more say in their education. "Students also need to learn to look for more effective behaviors while they wait, but they have less power over their lives than adults and little confidence that the school will change for the better. If we can restructure schools so that they are more satisfying, we can expect many more students to be patient when they are frustrated" (Glasser, 1986, p. 55).

The power seeker will vent his or her frustration with the teacher and with other group members. The teacher may prevent power struggles by using some of the following strategies advocated by Bellanca and Fogarty (1991) and Curwin and Mendler (1988).

Tactics to Use with Power Seekers
- Don't grab the hook. Teachers should not fall into the power trap, especially in front of the class.
- Listen to the problem.
- Acknowledge the student's feelings.
- Privately acknowledge the power struggle.
- Do not embarrass students.
- Defuse the power play.
- Give the students choices (consequences).
- Create a social contract.
- Place the power seeker in a leadership role.
- Reinforce the positive leadership.

Students who seek power will often try to dominate cooperative groups. If they cannot control the class, the teacher, or the school, they might consider their group as their personal power base. Teachers should monitor the roles assigned to group members and make sure power seekers are fulfilling their assignment without trying to take control of the entire group. If the tasks are structured so that they allow a great deal of choice, creativity, and freedom, power seekers should be satisfied that they do, in fact, have some control over their lives. Therefore, they can learn how to develop positive leadership qualities rather than negative dictatorial traits.

The following diagram helps the student and the teacher analyze what can be done to prevent the power struggle, resolve the current problem, and prevent future power struggles. This graphic organizer can also be filled out by the entire cooperative group so it can try to solve its own problems without involving the teacher, administrator, or parents.

FOCUS STRATEGY:
Phases of a Power Struggle

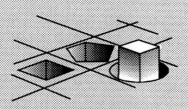

Strategy

The teacher and the student or students involved in the power struggle should fill out the causes of the conflict, what could have been done to prevent it, and how they can resolve the situation.

Analyze the power struggle to determine what proactive things could have been done to prevent the explosion, what caused the explosion, what steps could be taken to diffuse tempers, and possible resolutions to the problem.

Phases of a Power Struggle

Explosion Effect

Build up   **Cool down**

Causes

1. *Kim doesn't like the group*

2. *Kim feels Mary Ellen is bossy*

3. *Kim tells teacher she won't*

   work in group

Diffuse Temper

1. *Talk to Kim privately*

2. *Talk to other members of group*

3. *Talk to all members together*

   to discuss differences

Prevention

What could have been done
to prevent the problem?

1. *Mr. Love could have talked to Kim ahead*

   of time and told her about her new group

2. *Mr. Love could have made sure Kim*

   wasn't with the exact same group if she

   had had problems before

3. *All the students could have benefited*

   from a review of social skills

Resolution

Ways to resolve problem

1. *Discuss with whole group*

2. *Review social skills on conflict*

   resolution

3. *Monitor group closely*

4. *Make social contract with Kim*

5. *Talk to Mary Ellen about being bossy*

(Used with permission from Bob Wiedmann, The IRI Group)

OTHER POSSIBLE STRATEGIES TO USE

❑ **Keep it cool.** The power-seeking student often tries to excite and anger the teacher and fellow students. Remain calm.

❑ **Isolate the student from other group members or classmates.** Don't allow a confrontation to erupt where people say and do things they regret later.

❑ **Allow the student some time to cool down** and get herself together. Let her go to a private area to allow her to compose herself.

❑ **Defuse his anger** by saying, "I see your point," or "I know how you must feel," but then state the group rule that applies to all students.

❑ **Use a choice statement.** "At this point, you can join your assigned group or _____" (list consequences).

Possible consequences might include the following:

   a. **Go to the time-out area** to complete the assignment alone.
   b. **Receive an "F" or zero** on the assignment.
   c. **Meet with the group members** to discuss your differences.
   d. **Meet with students in the group individually** to work out personal problems.

❑ **Conference with the student** to find out if any personal or family problems are making him anxious or belligerent.

❑ **Find out the cause of the personality conflict between the student and the group.** Did they insult or embarrass her? Did they ignore her? Did they stifle her creativity? Did they assign her stupid tasks? Perhaps she has a legitimate complaint and it is the other group members who need help.

❑ **Write a contract with the student** to brainstorm alternative ideas he might try when he is upset and wants to take control of the group and/or the teacher.

❑ **Call the parents and talk to the counselor and other teachers** to find out if the student's outburst was unusual or if she is prone to seek power over other students or the teacher.

❑ **Try to give him a leadership position** in one of the next group activities. He can then exercise his leadership role in a positive rather than a negative way.

❑ **Reinforce anything the student does that is positive.** Encourage and praise her actions when she works cooperatively with others.

❑ **Consider pairing him with another strong student** so he will be forced to share power by alternating the power roles.

❑ **Have student keep a problem diary** and share with you what specific things upset her.

❑ **Assign him the role of observer** and have him keep track of the number of times people speak, what they say, and who is dominant, in order to keep him busy and involved.

Now Add Some of Your Own Solutions for Handling the Problem Described in the Scenario

❑ _____
_____
_____

❑ _____
_____
_____

❑ _____
_____
_____

❑ _____
_____
_____

❑ _____
_____
_____

❑ _____
_____
_____
_____

❑ _____
_____
_____
_____

❑ _____
_____
_____
_____

❑ _____
_____
_____
_____

❑ _____
_____
_____
_____

❑ _____
_____
_____
_____

❑ _____
_____
_____
_____

❑ _____
_____
_____
_____

❑ _____
_____
_____
_____

❑ _____
_____
_____
_____

❑ _____
_____
_____
_____

❑ _____
_____
_____
_____

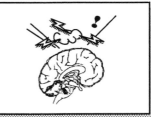

YOUR BRAINSTORMS …

Use the scenario at the beginning of this chapter or a similar problem scenario you have encountered to solve this problem and develop an action plan.

1   **Possible Quick-Recovery Solutions to the Problem**

_____
_____
_____

2   **Possible Next-Step Solutions**

_____
_____
_____

3   **Possible Long-Term Solutions**

_____
_____
_____

Rank Order the Solutions Within Each Classification

1 "QUICK RECOVERY"	**2** "NEXT STEP"	**3** "LONG TERM"
1._____ _____ _____ 2._____ _____ _____ 3._____ _____ _____	1._____ _____ _____ 2._____ _____ _____ 3._____ _____ _____	1._____ _____ _____ 2._____ _____ _____ 3._____ _____ _____

Explain *why* you ranked each solution first.

1 **Quick-Recovery Solution**

_____

_____

_____

2 **Next-Step Solution**

_____

_____

_____

3 **Long-Term Solution**

_____

_____

_____

Sequence the steps you will take to help solve this problem.

Step 1	Step 2	Step 3

Step 4	Step 5	Step 6

SKYLIGHT
PUBLISHING, INC.

Assess the effectiveness of your action plan:

_____

_____

_____

_____

_____

How will you celebrate your success?:

_____

_____

_____

_____

Reflect on a similar behavior problem you have had, review how you handled the problem at the time, and speculate about what you would do differently if you encounter the same problem again.

Problem:

_____

_____

_____

_____

What you did:

_____

_____

_____

_____

What you would do in the future:

_____

_____

_____

_____

19

Students Who Seek Revenge

"I'll show you who is in control"

As the students move their desks to get into their task groups, Bill shushes his group members.

"Okay, you guys, are we ready to give our presentation this afternoon?"

"Judy, you'll report on Hemingway's early life in Paris. Bobby will report on his literary style. Tim will report on his role as a bull fighter, a big game hunter, and a military man."

"Okay, let's get our notes and audiovisuals together. We only have about ten minutes to rehearse."

"This stinks," mumbles Bobby. *"I don't want to report on his style—that's boring. I want to talk about his love of bull fights and his big game hunting in Africa—that's cool!"*

"You can't," says Tim. *"I'm reporting on that. Besides, you were the one assigned to research his style. I don't know anything about it."*

A few minutes later Mrs. Voss calls on the group to give its presentation. Judy shows pictures of Hemingway as a young man in Paris and tells about his relationships with Gertrude Stein and F. Scott Fitzgerald.

It is now Bobby's turn to talk about Hemingway's style. Bobby walks to the front of the room and begins his talk to the class.

"Hemingway loved to go to the bullfights in Spain. Every year he and his friends would go to the running of the bulls, and then they would stay for the entire bull-fighting season....Here are some pictures of men being scared as they ran with the bulls..."

Tim stares straight ahead and begins to sweat profusely.

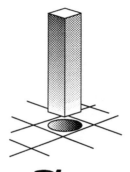

The Challenge

STUDENTS WHO SEEK REVENGE

Sometimes power seekers who never satisfy their need for power become revenge seekers to "get back" at the person or persons who thwarted their quest for power. Usually the revengeful student is trying to retaliate for something hurtful said by a parent, teacher, or peer or for some injustice or "unfair" deed.

The most important thing the teacher must do for the student who is seeking revenge is to help him or her form positive relationships through cooperative trust-building activities and other "bonding" activities. The social skill of encouragement needs to be emphasized, and the teacher should monitor group activities to make sure the revenge seeker is included.

Tactics to Use with Revenge Seekers

- Don't use sarcasm or put-downs.
- Don't confront student in front of his or her peers.
- Don't try to get revenge on revenge seekers.
- Listen carefully to their problems.
- Form a positive relationship with the student.
- Encourage the student.
- Build self-esteem.
- Process emotions positively.
- Have the student use journal writing to process feelings.
- Make sure everyone is included in all group activities.
- Use frequent teacher-student conferences to monitor behavior.

Revenge seekers need to be defused or else their "hidden agenda" may "torpedo" the group's effort. The other group members can then become resentful and distrustful of the revenge seeker. As a result, the revenge seeker compounds his or her personal problems by alienating peers and the teacher.

The hidden agenda can snowball into a personality problem that could brand the student as a "bully," "incorrigible," or a "loner" for the rest of the year or the rest of his or her schooling. Teachers need to take the time from the textbook and curriculum to allow students to process their emotions. If the students are not happy, satisfied, and accepted in the classroom, they will continue to disrupt learning and interfere with group interactions until their personal needs are met.

Sometimes students who seek revenge are not aware of their own motivations for their actions. The actions of Bobby in the scenario can be interpreted on many levels. He could be trying to get revenge on Tim by stealing his topic for his report. He could also just be very insecure about his own topic and his insecurity rather than revenge is what caused him to talk about Hemingway's love of bullfighting rather than his assigned topic of Hemingway's style. Bobby might benefit from keeping a divided journal where he comments on his own actions on the left column and then at a later date reflects on his actions in the right column.

FOCUS STRATEGY:
Reflective Divided Journal

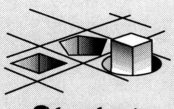

Ask students who seek revenge to describe what they think is happening. After they write the description, ask them to wait a short while and then reflect again on what happened.

Strategy

Name: *Bobby Gotcha*

Date: *March 18*

Name: *Bobby Gotcha*

Date: *March 22*

Description of Action	**Upon Reflection**
I had wanted to read about Hemingway's love of bullfighting because I had read *Death in the Afternoon* by him and I really loved it. When the group was deciding on topics, I was the last to pick. I was mad that I got the topic of Hemingway's style because style is boring and no one wanted it. I didn't want to look stupid in front of the class talking about style, so when I saw I went before Tim, I had a sudden urge to talk about what I knew best—so I did!	Well, Tim is still not talking to me and now our teacher found out, and she is subtracting points from my speech and she's going to call my mom. My whole group ignores me. I guess it was pretty dumb to think I could get away with it. I know now how embarrassed Tim was when he was called on to report on something he knew very little about. He really looked stupid trying to talk about Hemingway's style. I know I would be mad if someone did it to me. I think I'll talk to him and see what I can do to patch things up.

Signed: *Bobby G.*

Signed: *Bobby G.*

OTHER POSSIBLE STRATEGIES TO USE

❑ **Use I-messages:** "When I see you betraying the trust of your group, I feel upset."

❑ **Mediate a meeting between students** to find out why the behavior is occurring.

❑ **Have the group discuss the elements of trust and bonding** that are necessary for successful group work and discuss what the student can do to restore their trust in her.

❑ **Review social skills lesson on taking turns** so that the student understands that people do not always like their role or task, but everyone has to contribute his or her share.

❑ **Have the student work alone on his next project** until he can go back to the group with a promise to improve his cooperative skills.

❑ **Work out a social contract with the student** so that she counts to twenty, leaves the room, or goes to time-out whenever she thinks her temper might cause her to get even with someone in the group.

❑ Explore the student's motivation for revenge with a **school counselor or psychologist.**

Now Add Some of Your Own Solutions for Handling the Problem Described in the Scenario

❑ _____
_____
_____

❑ _____
_____
_____

❑ _____
_____
_____

❑ _____
_____
_____

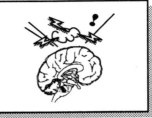

YOUR BRAINSTORMS ...

Use the scenario at the beginning of this chapter or a similar problem scenario you have encountered to solve this problem and develop an action plan.

1 **Possible Quick-Recovery Solutions to the Problem**

_____

_____

_____

2 **Possible Next-Step Solutions**

_____

_____

_____

3 **Possible Long-Term Solutions**

_____

_____

_____

Rank Order the Solutions Within Each Classification

1 "QUICK RECOVERY"	**2** "NEXT STEP"	**3** "LONG TERM"
1._____ _____ _____ 2._____ _____ _____ 3._____ _____ _____	1._____ _____ _____ 2._____ _____ _____ 3._____ _____ _____	1._____ _____ _____ 2._____ _____ _____ 3._____ _____ _____

SKYLIGHT PUBLISHING, INC.

Explain *why* you ranked each solution first.

1 **Quick-Recovery Solution**

_____

_____

_____

2 **Next-Step Solution**

_____

_____

_____

3 **Long-Term Solution**

_____

_____

_____

Sequence the steps you will take to help solve this problem.

Step 1	Step 2	Step 3

Step 4	Step 5	Step 6

SKYLIGHT PUBLISHING, INC.

Assess the effectiveness of your action plan:

_____

_____

_____

_____

_____

How will you celebrate your success?:

_____

_____

_____

_____

Reflect on a similar behavior problem you have had, review how you handled the problem at the time, and speculate about what you would do differently if you encounter the same problem again.

Problem:

_____

_____

_____

_____

What you did:

_____

_____

_____

_____

What you would do in the future:

_____

_____

_____

_____

20

Students With Aggressive Behaviors

Ms. Cox raises her hand to get the attention of the class. As soon as students raise their hands and focus their attention on her, she gives instructions for the next activity.

"Catch these scissors!"

"Today you are going to work in your base groups on a collage depicting positive social skills. The materials manager from
each group will pick up these magazines, a pair of scissors, a poster board, and some glue from the materials table and cut out three pictures the group selects. The organizer will monitor the time. You have thirty minutes for this activity. The recorder will write down why you selected a particular picture for your collage, and the last person in the group will be encourager."*

"All right," says Ms. Cox. *"You all have your roles and you know the assignment and the time limit. You may begin."*

Billy is the materials manager in his group, but he just sits there while everyone else is getting their magazines, scissors, and glue.

"Come on Billy," says Alice, *"Go get our stuff."*

Reluctantly, Billy gets up and goes to the table to get the supplies. Along the way he pokes Jim, steps on Mary Ann's feet, and knocks the magazines on to the floor.

"Okay, here is your stuff," he says sarcastically, as he tosses the scissors at Alice. The scissors graze Alice's arm and then fall in her lap.

"You could have hurt me," she cries and begins to run toward the teacher. *"I'm telling Ms. Cox. No one wants you in this group. You're weird."*

"I should have aimed better," Billy mutters sullenly as Ms. Cox begins to walk across the classroom with Alice hot on her heels.

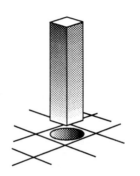

The Challenge

STUDENTS WITH AGGRESSIVE BEHAVIORS

A disinterested student rarely has a satisfying picture of school in his head; perhaps he has the picture of spending his days on the street 'hanging out.' But if his parents are able to force him to go to school, he may choose the angry behavior of disrupting to the extent that he is suspended. Now, out on suspension, he is satisfied. In school he was frustrated and he disrupted to get closer to the picture that he wants. On the street he is in control; in school he has almost no effective control at all. (Glasser, 1986, p. 53)

Students who display aggressive behavior are often trying to gain control over their lives. When students constantly utilize anger in an attempt to dominate other students or the group, they are incapable of finding a workable solution to their problems. Their inability to communicate causes them to try to overpower, intimidate, or hurt. If students are taught to disagree with the idea not the person, to negotiate, to discuss, and to compromise, aggressive behavior can be prevented. Anger can either be talked out or acted out. When students act out anger, aggression can be the result.

One strategy that can be used to help students monitor their own behavior is to meet with the student and discuss the idea of keeping an observation checklist on his or her own behaviors. At the end of the week the student should meet with the teacher to reflect on what days of the week are best and worst for the student and what areas he or she needs to improve. If a student has a chronic behavior problem, he or she should keep an observation sheet broken into hours for one day at a time. The teacher can also keep a checklist to record student behaviors.

FOCUS STRATEGY:
Behavior Observation Checklist

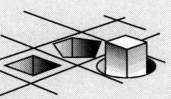

Strategy

Talk with the student to decide what type of behaviors need to be monitored. Ask the student to keep track of his or her own violations and answer the questions about his or her behavior before the conference.

Student: _Billy Scissorhands_   Date: _October 31_

Behavior	Mon.	Tues.	Wed.	Thurs.	Fri.	Total
Verbal Put-Downs	ЖЖ	III	II	I	ЖЖ III	19
Swearing	ЖЖ II	IIII	IIII	III	ЖЖ ЖЖ	28
Kicking	III	II	ЖЖ	II	IIII	16
Taking Things	II	IIII	IIII	II	ЖЖ I	18
Talking Loudly	ЖЖ I	III	III	II	ЖЖ	19
Touching or Pushing	IIII	II		III	III	12
TOTAL	27	18	18	13	36	

What day do you have the *fewest* behavior problems? _Thursday._

Why do you think you are better on that day? _Because we are usually reviewing for tests the next day_
and I know I better pay attention if I want to pass.

What day do you have the *most* behavior problems? _Friday._

Why do you think you behave poorly on that day? _Because I flunk most of the tests anyway._

What negative behavior do you use the most? _Swearing._

Why? _Because I get so angry with everybody calling me names because I'm so dumb._

What can you do to improve your behavior? _Maybe I can be nicer to my group members. They can_
help me study for tests. Then I can do better.

OTHER POSSIBLE STRATEGIES TO USE

❑ **Talk privately with the student** to find out why he behaves so aggressively with the other students. Ask him to come up with a solution. Let him know you think positively of him and are confident he can succeed.

❑ **Call the student's parents** and find out if she has displayed any aggressive tendencies at home or in other school situations and discuss possible solutions and follow-up conferences.

❑ **Talk with the school counselor** to see if there are any previous behavior problems on his record. See if a special education class or special counseling is warranted.

❑ **Give the student the option of going to the "time-out" or satellite area to work on her own.** She would be responsible for all work, but she would do it individually without assistance from the group.

❑ **Set up a verbal or non-verbal signal** that gives the student a warning that he is losing control. For example, one hand across another showing he has "crossed the line."

❑ **Discuss the behaviors of the other students in the base group with the student** to see if she is particularly aggravated by one of them and is therefore "acting out" because of a personality conflict.

❑ **Build a personal relationship with the student** by talking with him and discovering his special interests.

❑ **Evaluate her academic status to see if she feels inadequate** and is resorting to aggressive behavior to compensate for her inability to keep up with the rest of the group.

❑ **Change the base group** and place him with students with whom he can co-exist.

❑ **Have students keep a checklist** to keep track of their own anti-social behaviors—conference with them at the end of the period, day, or week.

❑ **Videotape a class and play it back to the student** to let her see how other people perceive her behavior.

❑ **Have the student keep a journal or log** where he writes about how he feels when he is upset or angry.

❑ **Assign her a role and task in which she will succeed** to increase her self-esteem.

❑ **While reviewing social skills, role play a simulated incident involving an aggressive situation** and have a discussion about how students should handle the problem.

Now Add Some of Your Own Solutions for Handling the Problem Described in the Scenario

❑ _____
_____
_____

❑ _____
_____
_____

❑ _____
_____
_____

❑ _____
_____
_____

❑ _____
_____
_____

❑ _____
_____
_____

❑ _____
_____
_____

❑ _____
_____
_____

❑ _____
_____
_____

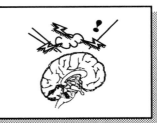

YOUR BRAINSTORMS ...

Use the scenario at the beginning of this chapter or a similar problem scenario you have encountered to solve this problem and develop an action plan.

1 **Possible Quick-Recovery Solutions to the Problem**

_____

_____

_____

2 **Possible Next-Step Solutions**

_____

_____

_____

3 **Possible Long-Term Solutions**

_____

_____

_____

Rank Order the Solutions Within Each Classification

1	**2**	**3**
"QUICK RECOVERY"	**"NEXT STEP"**	**"LONG TERM"**
1._____	1._____	1._____
_____	_____	_____
_____	_____	_____
2._____	2._____	2._____
_____	_____	_____
_____	_____	_____
3._____	3._____	3._____
_____	_____	_____
_____	_____	_____

Explain *why* you ranked each solution first.

1 **Quick-Recovery Solution**

_____

_____

_____

2 **Next-Step Solution**

_____

_____

_____

3 **Long-Term Solution**

_____

_____

_____

Sequence the steps you will take to help solve this problem.

Step 1	Step 2	Step 3

Step 4	Step 5	Step 6

SKYLIGHT PUBLISHING, INC.

Assess the effectiveness of your action plan:

_____

_____

_____

_____

_____

How will you celebrate your success?:

_____

_____

_____

_____

Reflect on a similar behavior problem you have had, review how you handled the problem at the time, and speculate about what you would do differently if you encounter the same problem again.

Problem:

_____

_____

_____

_____

What you did:

_____

_____

_____

_____

What you would do in the future:

_____

_____

_____

_____

21

Students Who Feel Inadequate

"I can't do this"

The students sit at their computer while Mr. Laylaw finishes giving instructions.

"Okay, each group is responsible for completing its final paper using the computer. Make sure you include all your footnotes and a bibliography."

"Today, the students who drew the role of 'Keyboard Operator' will be typing while the 'Researcher' finishes writing and the 'Proofreader' proofs the final product. You have until the end of the period to finish."

"I hate computers," Ginny exclaims. *"I don't even know how to boot the stupid system!"*

"You can do it," Chuck assures her. *"Just follow those step-by-step instructions we got last week."*

"File not found!" wails Ginny. *"I think I lost everything we did yesterday. I hate machines."*

"Okay, relax," Mary says. *"Just list the files again and we'll look for our title."*

"No, somebody else needs to work the keyboard," says Ginny as she gets up from the chair and walks away. *"I could never work the computer before; I can't work it now; and I'll never be able to work it. I'll just take an 'F,' and you guys can do it on your own. I'll never use the computer again."*

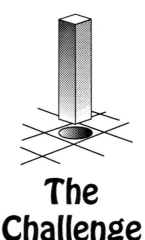

The Challenge

STUDENTS WHO FEEL INADEQUATE

Underachievers may seek attention, power, or revenge, but they all have underlying feelings of inadequacy. (Dinkmeyer, McKay, and Dinkmeyer, 1980, p. 253)

Students often play the "I can't" game because they feel they cannot accomplish the task perfectly. Some "inadequate" students need to realize that it's okay to be imperfect. They can still cooperate with others, perform tasks reasonably well, and produce products that are acceptable.

Dinkmeyer and Losoncy (1980) say that inadequate students often say "I can't," but what they really mean is "I won't." "I can't" is a form of passive resistance whereas "I won't" is a form of active resistance that usually provokes a power struggle or challenge to teachers. "The 'I can't' phrase suggests helplessness and can serve the following purposes:

1. One believes others should serve him or her and puts others in service by proclaiming inadequacy.
2. One believes that he or she is an inadequate person and protects himself or herself from possible failure by 'copping out'—avoiding facing life's challenges.
3. One believes that he or she is unable, helpless, and should be excused from being expected to function."

(Dinkmeyer and Losoncy, 1980, p. 55-56)

Often students who feel inadequate lack confidence in their ability and perceive life as "unfair" because they may try very hard, but their efforts still lead to failure. These students become discouraged and develop negative self-concepts. In some cases, the students totally withdraw and give up completely (Dinkmeyer and Losoncy, 1980). Teachers often let these quiet and withdrawn students "slip through the cracks" because they are too busy devoting their attention to the noisier students. Unfortunately, the discouraged and inadequate block of students is much larger than most people realize, and these "quiet" students often become dropout statistics.

Tactics to Use with Students Who Feel Inadequate
- Assign tasks that the student can successfully complete.
- Talk with the student to find out why he or she feels inadequate.
- Pair the inadequate student with another empathetic student who is task-oriented.

- Lower the student's anxiety about mistakes.
- De-emphasize grades.
- Break larger tasks into smaller chunks.
- Encourage—Encourage—Encourage!
- Remind students of past successes.
- Use team-building activities to build trust among group members.
- Give extra recognition for individual contributions to the group.
- Arrange for homework buddies so the student gets additional help and support.
- Give positive feedback.
- Give specific praise when appropriate.
- Help the student remediate specific learning deficiencies that may be causing feelings of inadequacy.
- Listen empathetically to the student's concerns, fears, and frustrations.
- Structure highly motivating group activities so the student is working toward a goal.

(Bellanca and Fogarty, 1991)

Some students who feel inadequate come to teachers with their "pessimistic expectations" ingrained in them since early childhood. Teachers should not expect to lift the heavy weight from their shoulders after only one or two challenging and successful group activities.

Persistence is the key to orchestrating group activities so that the student who feels inadequate can successfully fulfill his or her role, become a valuable member of the group, do well on total group activities, and succeed on individual tasks. These students will try to avoid anything that could cause them to fail; therefore, it's the obligation of the teacher to structure activities that will make the student succeed, gain confidence, and develop a positive self-concept.

Students need to identify the people and events that make them feel inadequate. If they keep a weekly log, they can chronicle their feelings and then decide how best to deal with the problems. They can also use the logs as a point of discussion with other students, the teacher, parents, or counselors.

FOCUS STRATEGY:
Weekly Behavior Log

Ask the student to keep a log to record the date and the incidents that make him or her feel inadequate. Meet with the student at the end of the week to analyze patterns and reflect on ways to increase self-esteem.

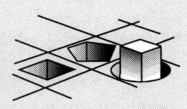

Strategy

Name: ___Ginny Lowtech___   Targeted Behavior: ___Develop confidence with computers___

1. Date: ___April 3___   Incident: ___I freaked out because I could not find my computer file. I blew up at my group.___

2. Date: ___April 5___   Incident: ___I asked to go to the "time-out" area to work on my own project because I was overwhelmed with the ideas the group decided on.___

3. Date: ___April 7___   Incident: ___I ran out of the room crying because I got a 67% on our computer programming test.___

4. Date: ___April 9___   Incident: ___I went to my counselor to see if I could drop my computer class. He said if I dropped this late in the course I'd get an "F."___

Reflection on Week: ___I'm not dumb! I just hate computers. I know I can help the group with spelling and writing, but I get so frustrated when I'm on the computer. I shouldn't have blown up at my group members because they were trying to help me.___

Plan for Next Week: ___I'm going to admit to the group how nervous I get around computers and ask for their help. Instead of running away from the problem, I am determined to beat that machine!___

Specific Things I Can Try: ___- Ask my teacher for extra help after school___
___- Use my lunch period to catch up on my work.___

© 1992 Skylight Publishing

OTHER POSSIBLE STRATEGIES TO USE

❑ **Use an activity called the "Me Bag"** where a pair of students exchange small lunch bags filled with things that describe them. Students have a chance to include items they are most proud of. The students then introduce each other to the class using the artifacts in the bag.

❑ **Work out a secret system with the inadequate student.** Promise the student you will only call on him if you are standing right next to him. That way the student does not have to worry about being called on at other times and can concentrate on the lesson.

❑ **Give the inadequate students a great deal of wait time when you ask questions.** Also, try to ask questions you know she can answer in order to build her confidence.

❑ **Give specific praise for the student's accomplishment.** In other words, don't just say "great speech." Tell the student the speech was great because he used good eye contact, effective gestures, and appropriate humor.

❑ **Make sure to allow enough time for each activity.** Inadequate students often feel rushed, and they become frustrated when the teacher and the class are moving "faster" than they are.

❑ **Leave some time between activities so students can "make the transition."** Often inadequate students suffer from learning disabilities also, and they have a difficult time changing their mind set quickly from one task to another.

❑ **Make sure all the homework assignments are realistic.** Do not give excessive amounts of homework because inadequate students get very frustrated when they cannot complete the work. It often takes them longer than other students.

❑ **Do not give new material for homework since students will not understand the new concepts.** The homework should be a review of concepts already studied.

**Now Add Some of Your Own Solutions for Handling the Problem
Described in the Scenario**

❑ _____
_____
_____

❑ _____
_____
_____

❑ _____
_____
_____

❑ _____
_____
_____

❑ _____
_____
_____

❑ _____
_____
_____

❑ _____
_____
_____

❑ _____
_____
_____

❑ _____
_____
_____

❑ _____
_____
_____

❑ _____
_____
_____

❑ _____
_____
_____

❏ _____
_____
_____

❏ _____
_____
_____

❏ _____
_____
_____

❏ _____
_____
_____

❏ _____
_____
_____

❏ _____
_____
_____

❏ _____
_____
_____

❏ _____
_____
_____

❏ _____
_____
_____

❏ _____
_____
_____

❏ _____
_____
_____

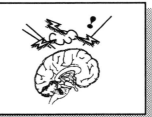

YOUR BRAINSTORMS …

Use the scenario at the beginning of this chapter or a similar problem scenario you have encountered to solve this problem and develop an action plan.

1 **Possible Quick-Recovery Solutions to the Problem**

_____

_____

_____

2 **Possible Next-Step Solutions**

_____

_____

_____

3 **Possible Long-Term Solutions**

_____

_____

_____

Rank Order the Solutions Within Each Classification

1	**2**	**3**
"QUICK RECOVERY"	**"NEXT STEP"**	**"LONG TERM"**
1._____	1._____	1._____
_____	_____	_____
_____	_____	_____
2._____	2._____	2._____
_____	_____	_____
_____	_____	_____
3._____	3._____	3._____
_____	_____	_____
_____	_____	_____

Explain *why* you ranked each solution first.

1 **Quick-Recovery Solution**

_____

_____

_____

2 **Next-Step Solution**

_____

_____

_____

3 **Long-Term Solution**

_____

_____

_____

Sequence the steps you will take to help solve this problem.

| Step 1 | Step 2 | Step 3 |

| Step 4 | Step 5 | Step 6 |

SKYLIGHT PUBLISHING, INC.

Assess the effectiveness of your action plan:

_____

_____

_____

_____

_____

How will you celebrate your success?:

_____

_____

_____

_____

Reflect on a similar behavior problem you have had, review how you handled the problem at the time, and speculate about what you would do differently if you encounter the same problem again.

Problem:

_____

_____

_____

_____

What you did:

_____

_____

_____

_____

What you would do in the future:

_____

_____

_____

_____

© 1992 Skylight Publishing

STUDENTS WITH SPECIAL NEEDS

REGULAR EDUCATION STUDENT

STUDENT WITH LEARNING CHALLENGES

WHAT THEY HAVE IN COMMON

Can memorize and recall important facts.

Usually develops academic achievement evenly.

Usually gets along well with peers.

Can read or write at grade level.

Does fairly well in all subjects.

Can stay on task most of the time.

Is usually organized.

Can arrange ideas sequentially.

Is usually physically coordinated.

Can usually follow oral and/or visual directions.

Wants to learn.

Wants to be liked by peers, parents, and teachers.

Wants to belong.

Wants to be successful.

Wants to pass.

Wants to graduate.

Has problems with short-term and long-term memory.

May develop academic achievement unevenly.

Sometimes has difficulty relating to peers.

Has problems in language areas (listening, speaking, reading, writing).

May have specific gaps in skills, such as spelling or math.

Is easily distracted at times.

May lack organizational skills.

May have difficulty following or creating a sequence.

May have coordination problems.

May have difficulty following oral directions.

(Adapted from Board of Education for the City of Etobicoke Writing Committee, 1987)

Students With Special Needs

The Regular Education Initiative (R.E.I.)

The trend in education in the 1990s is away from separate classes or separate programs and facilities for students with learning challenges, behavior problems, or handicaps. Pull-out programs for students who have been identified as having special learning and behavior problems are being eliminated in favor of placing all students in the regular education classrooms and getting them additional help from special education teachers or aides within the classrooms.

In 1975, Congress passed the Education for All Handicapped Children Act (EAHCA), more often referred to as P. L. 94-142. This federal incentive program was designed for the states to provide a comprehensive and consistent "specialized" education to children with handicaps. Often this "specialized" education took the form of "pull-out programs" where students were removed from the regular classroom settting and given additional help by the special education teacher. Research by Wang and Reynolds (1985) and others questions the classification system used to define special education and handicapped students. The research also supports a more powerful mainstreaming system with a full continuum of services and supplementary aids in the regular classes to enhance learning for *all* students—not just those classified as special education students.

"We believe that special education must be understood in terms of the whole educational enterprise. For the most part, general educators have not performed well in adapting to the varying needs of students—including, and especially, those students who present the most challenging learning problems. The result has been a mushrooming of many of the current special education and compensatory education programs" (Wang & Reynolds, 1985, p. 501).

A report issued in 1986 by the Assistant Secretary for Special Education and Rehabilitative Services for the United States Department of Education entitled "Educating Students with Learning Problems—A Shared Responsibility" calls for changes in the present delivery system for mildly handicapped children and children being served in compensatory programs like Chapter 1. The Regular Education Initiative (R.E.I.) criticizes the "pull-out" system of removing students from the regular classroom to get special help rather than coordinating regular education and special education into a full continuum of delivery services.

Glasser (cited in Gough, 1987) and others have also been critical of special programs for the "learning disabled." Glasser identifies "learning disabled" as "a group of students whose major disability is that they do not see school or education as need-satisfying" (p. 662). He also says that schools are spending a disproportionate amount of money trying to educate students who choose not to work in school, and the proliferation of special education programs is not going to help them. Dinkmeyer, McKay, and Dinkmeyer (1980) also suggest that many learning problems can be addressed by more effective teaching, better individualized instruction, more emphasis on students' self-concept, and efforts to increase students' self-esteem by making sure they are successful. Teachers today need to address the special needs of students who experience different types of learning challenges.

Many teachers feel that students with learning challenges resist learning because they just don't want to learn. Therefore, teachers treat the resistance as a form of negative behavior, thereby creating resentment, anger, and more serious discipline problems. Often, students with learning challenges do become students with behavior problems because they are struggling to establish their self-worth. Sometimes they try to control situations by arguing with other students or the teacher, blaming everyone but themselves for their problems, becoming defensive about their actions, or fighting with anyone about anything. They often try to control every situation because they live in constant fear of rejection, defeat, or failure. They have to be on guard constantly to defend their self-worth the best way they know how (Dinkmeyer, McKay, & Dinkmeyer, 1980).

Students with learning challenges can work to their capabilities if teachers give clear and concise directions, vary activities, establish clear classroom guidelines, and allow students to learn social interchange through group work. In group work students can learn the social skills necessary to change their behavior and function effectively in life (Dinkmeyer, McKay, & Dinkmeyer, 1980). Working in a group also helps students learn responsibility. Learning challenged students may be disorganized and always lose their worksheets, homework, notebook, pens, and books, but they can learn from other students when they model organizational skills and appropriate social skills. "Since all behavior has social meaning and is strongly influenced by the reactions of others, the group provides an excellent setting for bringing about change" (Dinkmeyer, McKay, & Dinkmeyer, 1980, p. 249).

By learning to work cooperatively in groups, students with special needs learn how to behave appropriately. Other group members can point out unacceptable behaviors, they can encourage students to succeed, they can compliment improvement, and they can encourage and praise good behavior. The use of group projects and group grades also helps students experience success because challenged students often become very discouraged and lose their self-esteem when they compare their performance with that of others.

Students with learning challenges will present special challenges to teachers. Being able to understand why certain students act the way they do and being able to address their academic and social needs will help teachers reduce the number of behavior problems that could occur in mainstreamed classes.

It should be noted that the students described in this section represent challenges for the teacher over which the students themselves have little or no control. Therefore, these students ought not to be considered "discipline problems," but rather students for whom the traditional classroom does not always work. That is not to say that a child with physical or language challenges may not *also* present other challenges described in this book, but it is useful to make the distinction between a "discipline problem" and a "learning challenge."

22

Students With Learning Challenges

"But I don't understand this!"

Bernice, Joyce, and Marcus quietly move their desks together as they begin their group assignment.

"Okay, you guys," starts Bernice. *"Since I'm the organizer we need to brainstorm examples of the different parts of speech for our matrix. We need to come up with six nouns, six pronouns, six verbs, six adverbs, and six adjectives and we only have five minutes. You're the recorder, Marcus. Let's get started."*

Bernice and Joyce start rattling off nouns, pronouns, and verbs, but Marcus, the recorder, is having a hard time writing everything down. He appears frustrated and seems on the verge of tears.

"What's wrong?" asks Joyce impatiently. *"We're doing all the thinking. All you have to do is write."*

Marcus continues to try to write what the girls are saying, but his writing becomes messier, his spelling is incorrect, and it is evident he has no idea what parts of speech each of the words are.

"What are we going to do?" Joyce asks Bernice in a low voice. *"He's really going to slow us up when we have to create sentences from our matrix. How are we supposed to do well when we always get stuck with a 'Sped' in our group?"*

Marcus breaks into tears, throws down his marker, and runs to the teacher. *"May I get a pass to see Mrs. Saunders, my resource teacher? I need to talk to her now!"*

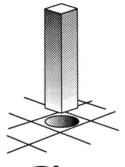

The Challenge

STUDENTS WITH LEARNING CHALLENGES

Students with learning challenges often experience frustration, anxiety, and tension when confronted with tasks that overwhelm them. Teachers who talk too fast, fire questions at students without giving adequate wait time, make comments that embarrass students, and intimidate students by yelling at them in front of their peers cause many students with learning challenges to withdraw from class interactions.

The learning-challenged student often has problems with processing language, visual perception, reading comprehension, and visual-motor coordination. They are often dyslexic; therefore, they are not able to decode information as quickly as others can. They also have a difficult time listening and taking notes at the same time. Moreover, they are better able to understand a written passage if they have heard it read by someone or have listened to it on an audio tape.

Students who have problems in the traditional classroom setting will probably have similar problems when they move into cooperative groups. Efforts must be made to structure activities and group interactions so that students with learning challenges can perform what is required, succeed in the task, and feel good about themselves.

One activity that helps group members bond together is to have the group complete a T-chart on the social skill of encouraging or energizing the group. Hopefully, the T-chart will help the other group members focus on positive reinforcement so that everyone in the group encourages one another.

FOCUS STRATEGY:
T-Chart

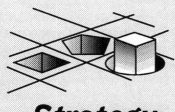

Strategy

Have the students in the group fill out a T-chart on "Encouraging Each Other." Have them discuss the importance of making each person feel special or welcome in the group.

ENCOURAGING EACH OTHER

Looks Like	**Sounds Like**
• Encouraging smiles and nods	"You can do it."
• Involvement of entire group	"Great idea."
• Active participation	"Way to go!"
• Sharing of ideas	"Awesome!"
• Active brainstorming	"How about this idea?"
• Eye-to-eye contact	"What do you think?"
• Sharing of materials	"Maybe I can help you."
• Students having fun	"Go for it."
• Students giving high-fives	"Thanks for your help."

OTHER POSSIBLE STRATEGIES TO USE

❑ **Structure activities so that the student gets assigned a less challenging role** (materials manager, observer, or encourager) so he can achieve some successes.

❑ **Put the student in a cooperative pair** with another student who is patient, supportive, and nurturing.

❑ **Review with the entire class the social skill of encouragement.**

❑ **Assign a new role,** of "Dictionary Person" for example, to help with the spelling of words.

❑ **Place the student with a hand-picked supportive group** for a few activities.

❑ **Assign a task where the student can showcase any special skills** (art, music, computer) so the student can earn the respect of the group members.

❑ **Talk with the student** about specific areas of academic weaknesses and ways to compensate for them.

❑ **Talk with the special education teacher** about strategies to use with the student and for the entire class.

❑ **Assign a peer tutor or "homework buddy"** to help the student catch up with the class.

❑ **Call the parents** to discuss the student's prior educational problems or to learn any tips they might have for helping the student achieve academic and social success.

Now Add Some of Your Own Solutions for Handling the Problem Described in the Scenario

❑ _____
_____
_____

❑ _____
_____
_____

❑ _____
_____
_____

❑ _____
_____
_____

❑ _____
_____
_____

❑ _____
_____
_____

❑ _____
_____
_____
_____

❑ _____
_____
_____

❑ _____
_____
_____

❑ _____
_____
_____

❑ _____
_____
_____

❑ _____
_____
_____

❑ _____
_____
_____

❑ _____
_____
_____

❑ _____
_____
_____

❑ _____
_____
_____

❑ _____
_____
_____

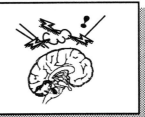

YOUR BRAINSTORMS …

Use the scenario at the beginning of this chapter or a similar problem scenario you have encountered to solve this problem and develop an action plan.

1 **Possible Quick-Recovery Solutions to the Problem**

_____
_____
_____

2 **Possible Next-Step Solutions**

_____
_____
_____

3 **Possible Long-Term Solutions**

_____
_____
_____

Rank Order the Solutions Within Each Classification

1 "QUICK RECOVERY"	**2** "NEXT STEP"	**3** "LONG TERM"
1._____	1._____	1._____
_____	_____	_____
_____	_____	_____
2._____	2._____	2._____
_____	_____	_____
_____	_____	_____
3._____	3._____	3._____
_____	_____	_____
_____	_____	_____

SKYLIGHT PUBLISHING, INC.

Explain *why* you ranked each solution first.

1 **Quick-Recovery Solution**

_____

_____

_____

2 **Next-Step Solution**

_____

_____

_____

3 **Long-Term Solution**

_____

_____

_____

Sequence the steps you will take to help solve this problem.

Step 1

Step 2

Step 3

Step 4

Step 5

Step 6

SKYLIGHT PUBLISHING, INC.

Assess the effectiveness of your action plan:

_____

_____

_____

_____

_____

How will you celebrate your success?:

_____

_____

_____

_____

Reflect on a similar behavior problem you have had, review how you handled the problem at the time, and speculate about what you would do differently if you encounter the same problem again.

Problem:

_____

_____

_____

_____

What you did:

_____

_____

_____

_____

What you would do in the future:

_____

_____

_____

_____

 SKYLIGHT PUBLISHING, INC.

© 1992 Skylight Publishing

23

Students With Behavior Challenges

"Give me that leaf or you're history!"

The students break into their cooperative science groups and begin examining different kinds of leaves and recording their observations.

Trina, Raul, and David pull their desks together. Trina begins looking at the first leaf while Raul checks off the characteristics of the leaf on the worksheet. David becomes impatient waiting for his turn.

He yells at Trina, *"Come on—quit taking so long. Give me the leaf."*

Trina ignores him and keeps talking about the leaf as Raul records her observations.

Suddenly, David reaches across the desk and rips the leaf from Trina's hand.

"Way to go," screeches Trina. *"Now you ripped it. How are we supposed to get anything done when you act like a spoiled brat?"*

"Who cares!" yells David. *"These leaves all look alike anyway. Big deal."*

"Shut up," says Raul. *"Just because you don't do your share, don't expect us to fail science too!"*

David becomes livid with anger. He tries to talk, but he can't form the words. Suddenly, he reaches across the table and grabs the bag of leaves. He jumps up, crumples all the leaves with his hands, and throws the small pieces at Raul's face.

"*Stuff it,*" screams David as he sits back in his seat.

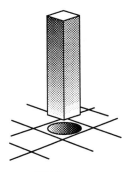

The Challenge

STUDENTS WITH BEHAVIOR CHALLENGES

Often, students with behavior challenges misbehave to cover up insecurity about a task. If the task is too complicated, difficult, or confusing, the student might resort to disruptive behavior when in reality, he or she just doesn't know what to do. Teachers who immediately send the misbehaving student to the time-out area or to the office without trying to discover the real problem might be unintentionally encouraging the behavior. The student doesn't want to be in the specific situation in the first place. If the teacher removes the student from the situation by sending him or her to time-out or to the office, the student never has to deal with the "real" problem. Teachers should observe the student to see when he or she becomes frustrated and perhaps simplify the task so he or she can feel successful. Social rewards of appreciation, praise, smiling, attention, and specific compliments will reinforce positive behaviors, raise the students' self-esteem, and encourage him or her to keep trying.

Teachers can use the conference as a tool to explore the student's problem and arrive at a compromise. Like everyone, students with behavior challenges want some choice in their lives, and a teacher can listen empathetically to the problem, help brainstorm ideas, and jointly explore possible solutions to problems. In addition, efforts should be made to discover whether the student's behavior is related to an academic problem. Many disruptive students try to camouflage their weak academic skills by developing a "tough" persona; they would be humiliated if their peers found out they couldn't read or write. Too often teachers react to the surface problem of misbehavior when the core problem is actually something else, such as feelings of inadequacy or frustration.

One strategy that could be used to chronicle the behavior of a student and seek patterns or causes is the Modified Case Study. A sample of the case study follows.

FOCUS STRATEGY:
Modified Case Study

The teacher of the student with chronic behavior problems should start documenting patterns of behavior and gathering background information to use with the students, the parents, and the administrator in a conference.

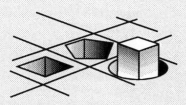

Strategy

POSITIVE DISCIPLINE AND MOTIVATION

Date: *January 13*   School: *Spring Elementary*   Grade: *5*
Student: *David Trouble*   Age: *11*   Teacher: *Mrs. Armstrong*

Briefly describe the problem the student is having in class
    David often loses his temper and does things that hurt other students. The other students resent his outbursts and do not want to work with him.

Log of specific behavior
    Date: *December 6*
    Incident: *David asked Jimmy to borrow a crayon. When Jimmy told David "No" because he was using the crayon, David punched Jimmy.*
    Date: *December 10*
    Incident: *David got frustrated when he couldn't answer his math problem and he tore up his worksheet.*
    Date: *December 15*
    Incident: *Mary Ann told David she didn't want him in her group. David turned over his chair and ran out of the room crying.*
    Date: *December 20*
    Incident: *David refused to work on his writing assignment. When I asked him to get to work, he put his head down on the desk.*

Pertinent Information from Permanent Files
    • *David was referred for testing in special education in the third grade.*
    • *David was held back in the fourth grade.*
    • *David was assigned to the Resource Room for two periods a day.*

Test Scores
    Iowa _____
    IGAP _____

Contact with parent
    12/7   *Talked with mother about David's fighting problem. The mother said he has been belligerent since the parents went through a divorce two years ago. She said she would talk to him, but he doesn't seem to listen to her.*
    12/16 *Had conference with mother to discuss David's poor grades. She promised to help him with his work.*

SKYLIGHT
PUBLISHING, INC.

FOCUS STRATEGY continued

Contact with counselor or administrator (ask about evaluations done by school psychologists or sociologoists)

12/17   Talked with school counselor. He said David has a problem accepting being pulled out of his regular fifth-grade class and going to the Resource Room. He feels embarrassed because all of his friends know he has a learning problem.

Conference with student

12/18   David says he feels intimidated by his group members because they are much smarter than he is. He says that is why he "acts out" and does wild things. We decided it would be best to change groups and put David with one other student. That way he will feel more involved with the decisions, and he will get some one-on-one tutoring from the other student.

Follow-up meeting
January 23

Teacher: _____Mrs. Armstrong_____
Student: _____David_____
Parent: _____Mr. Trouble_____

OTHER POSSIBLE STRATEGIES TO USE

❑ **Talk with the student** to find out why he doesn't get along with his group members. Ask the student what he thinks could be done to help him control his temper and get along better with others.

❑ **Use proximity** to let student feel your presence. If you stand nearby, you can observe activities, behaviors, or remarks that might lead to an outburst.

❑ **Talk to special education teacher** about strategies to use to help the student curb her desire for attention and aggressiveness toward her peers.

❑ **Allow student to complete work in "time-out" area** so he can work alone until he calms down.

❑ **Pair student** with a student who is supportive and nurturing.

❑ **Give the student a role like recorder or organizer** where she has to be the center of positive attention rather than negative attention.

❑ **Call parents** to see if personal or family problems could be making the student upset.

❑ **Check student's file** to see if low academic abilities may be causing him to compensate for his inadequacies by using aggression.

❑ **Keep a tally** of the times of the day and the types of activities that seem to cause the most aggravation and frustration for the student.

❑ **Review social skills** of listening, sharing, encouragement, and taking turns with entire class or with the student who is having problems.

Now Add Some of Your Own Solutions for Handling the Problem Described in the Scenario

❑ _____
_____
_____

❑ _____
_____
_____

❑ _____
_____
_____

❑ _____
_____
_____

❑ _____
_____
_____

❑ _____
_____
_____

❑ _____
_____
_____

❑ _____
_____
_____

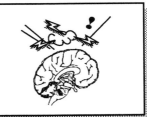

YOUR BRAINSTORMS ...

Use the scenario at the beginning of this chapter or a similar problem scenario you have encountered to solve this problem and develop an action.

1 **Possible Quick-Recovery Solutions to the Problem**

_____

_____

_____

2 **Possible Next-Step Solutions**

_____

_____

_____

3 **Possible Long-Term Solutions**

_____

_____

_____

Rank Order the Solutions Within Each Classification

1 "QUICK RECOVERY"	**2** "NEXT STEP"	**3** "LONG TERM"
1._____ _____ _____ 2._____ _____ _____ 3._____ _____ _____	1._____ _____ _____ 2._____ _____ _____ 3._____ _____ _____	1._____ _____ _____ 2._____ _____ _____ 3._____ _____ _____

Explain *why* you ranked each solution first.

1 **Quick-Recovery Solution**
_____
_____
_____

2 **Next-Step Solution**
_____
_____
_____

3 **Long-Term Solution**
_____
_____
_____

Sequence the steps you will take to help solve this problem.

Step 1	Step 2	Step 3

Step 4	Step 5	Step 6

SKYLIGHT
PUBLISHING, INC.

Assess the effectiveness of your action plan:

_____
_____
_____
_____
_____

How will you celebrate your success?:

_____
_____
_____
_____

Reflect on a similar behavior problem you have had, review how you handled the problem at the time, and speculate about what you would do differently if you encounter the same problem again.

Problem:

_____
_____
_____
_____

What you did:

_____
_____
_____
_____

What you would do in the future:

_____
_____
_____
_____

 SKYLIGHT PUBLISHING, INC.

Gifted Students

"I have a better idea"

"**S**tudents, you will be working in informal groups today to write a limerick about spring. You know your groups and your roles, so let's get started. Each group will read its poem to the class.

"*I forget the rhyme scheme of a limerick,*" Cheryl says.

"*It's a-a-b-b-a,*" says Josh. "*And there are nine syllables in the first, second, and fifth lines and six syllables in the third and fourth lines.*"

"*Let's do the first two lines,*" says Pam.

"*How about, 'There once was a robin named Spring, whose worm to his tree he did bring'!*" exclaims Ruth.

"*Why don't we use some onomatopoeia,*" interjects Josh.

"*Say what?!*" Cheryl laughs.

"*You know, words that actually sound like the way they are written,*" answers Josh. "*Like 'moo' or 'swish.'*"

"*No way,*" says Pam. "*Let's just do a simple limerick and get it over with.*"

"But I don't want to read a stupid worm poem to the whole class. I'll be embarrassed," exclaims Josh. *"Let's use some similes and metaphors—figurative language makes poetry come alive."*

"'Come alive'?" laughs Cheryl. *"'Figurative'—how can we use it if we can't 'figure it out'?"*

Everyone but Josh laughs.

"Okay," Josh says quietly. *"Do whatever you guys want."*

The group finishes its poem and reads it in front of the class.

Cheryl reads:

> *There once was a robin named Spring*
> *Whose worm to his tree he did bring.*
> *The worm twisted and wriggled*
> *The bird just giggled*
> *And then the robin began to sing.*

The class laughs when it hears the poem, but Josh turns beet red as he returns to his seat, disgusted.

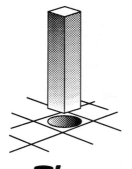

The Challenge

GIFTED STUDENTS

The parents and teachers of gifted students tend to argue for tracking students and using homogeneous groups in cooperative learning classrooms. Many people feel that the gifted students will end up doing all the work in mixed-ability groups, will be slowed down in their academic growth, and will not be exposed to the high-level enrichment activities usually reserved for homogeneously grouped classes. Often, however, heterogeneously mixed groups allow the gifted students to learn how to work with all types of students and how to practice their social skills.

Gifted students may possess such positive characteristics as an advanced vocabulary, a rich verbal background, and a high reading level. They also like to try new things and take risks, are sensitive to beauty, and can generate a large number of ideas or solutions to problems. When gifted students participate in group work they usually get absorbed in relevant topics, make value judgments, have a good sense of humor, and persist in completing tasks over extended periods. Negative characteristics can include getting bored doing routine tasks and tending to dominate the group by taking control in order to make sure the assignment is completed to their own high standards (Board of Education for the City of Etobicoke Writing Committee, 1987).

Gifted students still need help acquiring and maintaining their positive self-concepts because they often feel other students perceive them as being "different." They also have fears about living up to the high expectations their parents and teachers have for their future, and fears about fitting in socially with other class members.

Teachers have to structure group activities so that all students are challenged, exposed to creative evaluation experiences, and have an opportunity to express their talents. At the same time, teachers must ensure that students share the work, take turns, listen, respect the opinions of others, and abide by all the other social skills so that they learn how to function effectively in a heterogeneous group (Board of Education for the City of Etobicoke Writing Committee, 1987).

The K-W-L graphic organizer is one device that can be utilized to make sure that gifted students (and *all* students, for that matter) are encouraged to pursue additional interests and expand and extend their knowledge base. In the scenario, Josh obviously knew a great deal about poetry, and his higher-level poetic capabilities were not stretched when his group wrote the limerick about spring. Using the K-W-L chart, Josh can list all he knows about poetry in the "K" column, and list what he wants to know in the "W" column. The teacher could then encourage Josh to do additional research on poetry based on the things he wants to find out. He could research the topics, prepare a report, read more difficult peoms, and write some original poetry. He could also share some of his poetry with his group and the class and maybe serve as a resource person for future poetry units. After he completes his activities, he can fill in the last column "L" on what he has learned about poetry and receive recognition for his special accomplishments.

FOCUS STRATEGY:
K–W–L

Ask the student to fill out a K-W-L graphic organizer about a topic that he or she would like to explore further. Discuss potential research tasks and projects as well as what is "Learned" after completing the research.

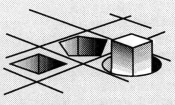

Strategy

Name of Student: *Josh Gifted*
Date: *April 3*
Title of Unit: *Poetry*

K What I Know	**W** What I Want to Know	**L** What I've Learned
limericks	*how to write a sonnet*	*There are two types of sonnets:*
similes	*how to write a haiku*	*- Shakespearean*
metaphors	*how to explicate a poem*	*- Petrarchan*
		how to write free verse
onomatopoeia	*how to write free verse*	*how to write a haiku*
hyperbole	*how to write an ode*	*how to explicate a poem*
rhyme scheme		
iambic pentameter		
quatrains		

Research Task: *I would really like to learn more about the sonnet. I know it is more difficult than the limerick, and I would like the challenge.*
Project: *I will research two types of sonnets and write a Shakespearean sonnet.*
Due Date: *April 10.*
Reflection: *The other students may not like the sonnet as well as the limerick, but I am proud of my accomplishment.*

Signed: *Josh Gifted*

OTHER POSSIBLE STRATEGIES TO USE

❑ Allow students to do **enrichment activities** in addition to their group assignments.

❑ **Make sure roles rotate frequently.** Often the gifted student will attempt to take over the group in order to get her ideas implemented.

❑ Allow students to **research ideas or explore creative options** so they do not get bored.

❑ Don't make gifted students do "more of the same" activities if they finish their work early. **Allow them to experiment with new ideas.**

❑ **Don't always make the gifted or advanced students help other students who do not understand the assignment.** Students do remember ninety-five percent of what they teach others, but they will become discouraged if they are always helping other students "catch up" rather than "moving forward" themselves.

❑ **Give the student positive attention** at times by letting him share what he knows with the class. (Perhaps Josh could have demonstrated "onomatopoeia" words for the whole class.)

Now Add Some of Your Own Solutions for Handling the Problem Described in the Scenario

❑ _____
_____
_____

❑ _____
_____
_____

❑ _____
_____
_____

❑ _____
_____
_____

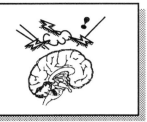

YOUR BRAINSTORMS ...

Use the scenario at the beginning of this chapter or a similar problem scenario you have encountered to solve this problem and develop an action plan.

1 **Possible Quick-Recovery Solutions to the Problem**

_____

_____

_____

2 **Possible Next-Step Solutions**

_____

_____

_____

3 **Possible Long-Term Solutions**

_____

_____

_____

Rank Order the Solutions Within Each Classification

1	**2**	**3**
"QUICK RECOVERY"	**"NEXT STEP"**	**"LONG TERM"**
1._____	1._____	1._____
2._____	2._____	2._____
3._____	3._____	3._____

SKYLIGHT PUBLISHING, INC.

Explain *why* you ranked each solution first.

1 **Quick-Recovery Solution**

_____

_____

_____

2 **Next-Step Solution**

_____

_____

_____

3 **Long-Term Solution**

_____

_____

_____

Sequence the steps you will take to help solve this problem.

Step 1	Step 2	Step 3

Step 4	Step 5	Step 6

SKYLIGHT
PUBLISHING, INC.

Assess the effectiveness of your action plan:

_____
_____
_____
_____
_____

How will you celebrate your success?:

_____
_____
_____
_____

Reflect on a similar behavior problem you have had, review how you handled the problem at the time, and speculate about what you would do differently if you encounter the same problem again.

Problem:

_____
_____
_____
_____

What you did:

_____
_____
_____
_____

What you would do in the future:

_____
_____
_____
_____

25

Students With Language Challenges

"No comprendo, amigo!"

"**J**ose, you will be in this group," Ms. Merrill says as she leads him to an empty seat next to James and Lee.

"James and Lee, I want you to meet a new member of your group. This is Jose who just moved here from Central America. He only knows a little bit of English so you will need to help him with our social studies project."

"Hi Jose, welcome," Lee says as he holds out his hand to shake hands with Jose.

"Hola," greets James with a misplaced accent. "Como estas, I think!"

As Ms. Merrill walks away, Lee whispers to James.

"How can he help us with our project? He can't read so he can't do the research."

"Yeah," James answers. "And since he can't speak English he can't help us with our presentation."

Jose smiles and sits down cautiously, oblivious to what Lee and James are saying.

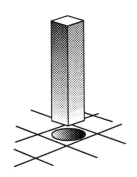

The Challenge

STUDENTS WITH LANGUAGE CHALLENGES

Group work offers a powerful tool to help students speak English proficiently and to help them acquire the basic skills and the higher-order thinking skills needed to perform academically.

Neves and Hatch (in Cohen, 1986) reviewed the literature and found that second-language learners need to work with peers in order to acquire the second language quickly. Therefore, if teachers construct what Cohen calls "rich tasks for group work" that contain active involvement, relevancy, pictures, role-playing, manipulatives, non-verbal cues, and realistic communicative situations, it is possible to place students who do not share a common language in the same group. Cohen suggests that mixed groups are preferable because the non-English-speaking student will benefit more if a proficient bilingual student is also in the group to help translate. "The bilingual child needs to be taught that he or she is a valuable bridge in the group, explaining to the monolinguals what the others are saying and offering special help to the non-English-speaking students" (Cohen, 1986, p. 133).

Neves (in Cohen, 1986) found that in classrooms where both languages were utilized by both teachers and children, bilingual students had the highest social status. They were often chosen on a socio-metric scale as "friends" to more students. Moreover, as the year progresses in a bilingual classroom, both English-speaking and non-English-speaking students begin to understand the other language, even if they are not able to speak it.

Group work can also help the older, limited-English-speaking students who entered an English-speaking school in first grade. Even though their English skills are good, they still are lacking many of the basic skills they should have learned in the early grades but they missed because of communication problems. Since many of the limited-English-speaking students are functioning several years behind grade level, they need the help of students in the group to help them catch up with the basic skills in the process of working on higher-order thinking projects. The bilingual or English-speaking students in the cooperative group can help by reading out loud, paraphrasing articles, summarizing key points, and reviewing important terms and materials. The support of a peer group and the verbal interaction among group members reinforces language. Cohen (1986) suggests that group work is preferable to pulling limited-English-speaking students out of regular classes and placing them in special ESL classes where they are unlikely to interact with English-speaking classmates. Arias (in Cohen, 1986) found that even within model bilingual classrooms that included English-speaking students, children were called on to recite formally, but then they were very quiet the rest of the class and were provided few or no opportunities to practice English informally with their peers. Mixing limited-English-speaking students in with heterogeneously mixed cooperative groups certainly presents many challenges for the students themselves, the other group members, and the teacher; however, Cohen (1991) states that "the multi-ability classroom permits teaching at a very high level despite the challenge of linguistic and academic diversity among the students" (p. 7). She further adds that teachers will need complex instruction strategies to bring about intellectual growth for all students.

The T-chart once again can be used to reinforce the social skills of communication. Students in the group can fill out a T-chart on the skill of "Making Sure Everyone Speaks." In order to be sure each student gets a chance to speak without being interrupted, have the person who is speaking hold a symbol like a stick, magic marker, or stuffed animal. Only the person with the "speaking symbol" is allowed to speak. Everyone else must listen until it is his or her turn to speak.

FOCUS STRATEGY:
T–Chart

Give a blank T-chart on the social skill of "Making Sure Everyone Speaks" to each group. Ask the students to discuss the importance of each idea when they add it to the list.

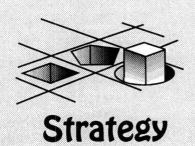

Strategy

MAKING SURE EVERYONE SPEAKS

Looks Like	Sounds Like
• eyes on speaker • speaker's symbol is rotated • checker keeps track of how often everybody speaks • group uses positive gestures • smiling • nodding	• one person speaks at a time • affirmations from listeners • others' opinions voiced • questions for speaker • positive verbal feedback • checker encourages everyone

OTHER POSSIBLE STRATEGIES TO USE

❑ **If there is a student in the class who is bilingual, put the non-English-speaking student in his or her group.**

❑ **Place the student in a group with someone who has studied his language in school.**

❑ **Find some reading materials or tapes in the student's language so that she feels like the teacher cares.**

❑ **Plan a lesson or unit around multi-cultural activities** so that the student has a chance to bring in native costumes, games, and sports to share with the rest of the class.

❑ **Place student with one other student who wants to learn his language** and provide the pair with a bilingual dictionary so that both students can practice learning a new language.

❑ **Organize the groups so that the student gets easier roles** like materials manager, encourager, or observer until she builds her confidence.

❑ **Arrange for after-school tutoring.**

❑ **Establish pen pals** from the student's home land for the class. The student can help edit the letters that go out and read the letters that arrive.

❑ **Learn some of the student's language and use it in class.**

❑ **Make bilingual posters** for group rules and consequences, social skills, and classroom procedures.

Now Add Some of Your Own Solutions for Handling the Problem Described in the Scenario

❑ _____
_____
_____

❑ _____
_____
_____

❑ _____
_____
_____

❑ _____
_____
_____

❑ _____
_____
_____

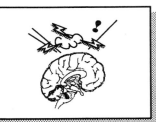

YOUR BRAINSTORMS ...

Use the scenario at the beginning of this chapter or a similar problem scenario you have encountered to solve this problem and develop an action plan.

1 **Possible Quick-Recovery Solutions to the Problem**

_____

_____

_____

2 **Possible Next-Step Solutions**

_____

_____

_____

3 **Possible Long-Term Solutions**

_____

_____

_____

Rank Order the Solutions Within Each Classification

1 "QUICK RECOVERY"	**2** "NEXT STEP"	**3** "LONG TERM"
1._____ _____ _____ 2._____ _____ _____ 3._____ _____ _____	1._____ _____ _____ 2._____ _____ _____ 3._____ _____ _____	1._____ _____ _____ 2._____ _____ _____ 3._____ _____ _____

SKYLIGHT PUBLISHING, INC.

Explain *why* you ranked each solution first.

1 **Quick-Recovery Solution**

_____

_____

_____

2 **Next-Step Solution**

_____

_____

_____

3 **Long-Term Solution**

_____

_____

_____

Sequence the steps you will take to help solve this problem.

Step 1	**Step 2**	**Step 3**

Step 4	**Step 5**	**Step 6**

SKYLIGHT
PUBLISHING, INC.

Assess the effectiveness of your action plan:

_____

_____

_____

_____

_____

How will you celebrate your success?:

_____

_____

_____

_____

Reflect on a similar behavior problem you have had, review how you handled the problem at the time, and speculate about what you would do differently if you encounter the same problem again.

Problem:

_____

_____

_____

What you did:

_____

_____

_____

What you would do in the future:

_____

_____

_____

_____

SKYLIGHT PUBLISHING, INC.

26

Students With Physical Challenges

"I can't keep up with the group"

"**W**e've got to rehearse our rap song," Edna calls out. "We only have twenty minutes before we present it to the class."

"Let's go out in the hall and practice our dance steps to make sure we have the routine down pat," adds Patrick.

As the group members file out into the hall, Helen sits in her wheelchair staring at them. She starts to wheel herself toward the door, but then reconsiders and rolls back to her desk. She waits for the group to return and then watches while they present their rap song and dance to the class.

The song is a big hit and the class breaks into wild applause as the group members finish the routine and return to her side.

"Wow, that was a lot of fun," says Edna.

"We were the best group in the class," exclaims Patrick.

"How did you like it, Helen?"

"It was great," replies Helen. "I only wish I could have gone up there with you."

"Well, you could have come up with us to sing—why didn't you?"

"I don't know why I didn't come up," answers Helen. *"Maybe it was because no one asked me!"*

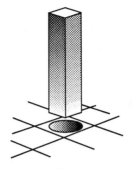

The Challenge

STUDENTS WITH PHYSICAL CHALLENGES

In the last fifteen years, schools have been moving away from segregated special education settings for children with intellectual, behavioral, and physical challenges toward the creation of inclusive classrooms. *Inclusive classrooms are those designed to meet the educational needs of all their members within a common environment.* (Sapon-Shevin, 1991, p. 8)

According to Stainbock and Stainbock, inclusive classrooms are based on three key principles.

1. All children are entitled to learn with their chronological age peers. Children do not have to earn the right to be in a "regular classroom...."

2. All children in a classroom need to be engaged in learning that is appropriate to their skills and needs....

3. All children need to take responsibility for helping each other to learn and grow....

(cited in Sapon-Shevin, 1991, p. 8)

Teachers will have the responsibility of teaching social skills to the special education students and the regular education students who will work with them. "Proponents of inclusive education believe that all children profit from learning in heterogeneous settings; learning about human interconnectedness, caring, and responsibility is as important as learning math, reading, and writing" (Sapon-Shevin, 1991, p. 8).

Cooperative learning, therefore, provides an ideal structure for integrating these students into the regular education classroom. All students need to learn how to recognize and accept individual differences because diversity enriches learning. As society becomes more multicultural, teachers must recognize that all students differ. Students cannot be divided into "typical" and "handicapped." Sapon-Shevin (1991) states, "Our students vary along many dimensions: race, class, gender, ethnicity, family background and make-up, religion, academic skills, motor skills, interests" (p. 10).

Students need to learn how to accept and to value diversity and participate in cooperative groups that prepare them to live in inclusive cooperative communities. Johnson and Johnson (cited in Tateyawa-Sniezek, 1990) feel that "learning situations should be structured cooperatively, not competitively or individualistically, to maximize the achievement of handicapped students" (p. 436).

The challenge facing teachers involves structuring group activities that allow physically challenged students to achieve their academic goals while at the same time cultivating, nurturing, and reinforcing the social skills that the research shows is necessary for their acceptance by regular-education students. Careful attention must be paid to the types of tasks given to groups, the roles assigned to each member, and the method of evaluation. Teachers need to be aware of what they can do to help the challenged student succeed and to structure authentic assessments to measure the performance and development of the student.

Most importantly, an atmosphere of trust and caring must be established in the classroom and an emphasis on social skills, cooperation, and understanding must permeate the learning environment if the challenged students are to fit into the cooperative learning classroom.

In the scenario at the beginning of the chapter, Helen needed to communicate with her group members. If a team has truly bonded, team members should be in tune with each other's feelings. Team members should also make allowances for each other's strengths. Maybe the group members were aware of Helen's feelings, but they didn't know how to handle the situation effectively. One strategy that could be used to make the group members aware of each other's capabilities is the Ranking Graphic Organizer. Each member of the group should "rank order" his or her strengths, discuss the strengths with the other group members, and refer to the lists whenever they plan group projects. They can also add to the lists when they discover new hidden talents or strengths. Open communication is the key to effective interpersonal relationships.

FOCUS STRATEGY:
Ranking Strengths

Give each member of the group a copy of the Ranking Graphic Organizer. Ask them to list their individual strengths. After everyone has completed their individual ranking, discuss strengths with the entire group.

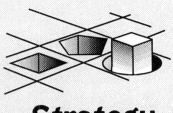

Strategy

Student: *Helen*   Team: *The Ninjas*   Date: *April 2*

List your strengths in any area (writing, art, music, speaking, organization, cooking, etc.)

Writing Poetry

Spelling

Singing

Art Work

Math

Public Speaking

Calligraphy

- Discuss your strengths with your fellow group members.

- File lists in your team notebook and review them before discussing team projects.

- Update individual lists as new talents or strengths emerge.

- Draw on the strengths of each team member when developing group projects.

© 1992 Skylight Publishing

OTHER POSSIBLE STRATEGIES TO USE

❑ **Monitor groups** more closely to make sure all students are included in group activities.

❑ **Review social skills** of including everyone in all activities, giving encouragement, and helping each other.

❑ **Talk to group members privately** and ask them to be aware of how they might feel if they were left out of a fun group activity because of a physical challenge.

❑ **Talk to the student** about ways she can assert herself more to make sure she contributes to the group effort.

❑ **Assign the student to a nurturing group** that will be sensitive to his needs as well as friendly and supportive.

❑ **Have students in the class role-play situations** that people who are blind, deaf, or physically challenged face each day so that they become more aware and sensitive to the needs of these students.

Now Add Some of Your Own Solutions for Handling the Problem Described in the Scenario

❑ _____
_____
_____

❑ _____
_____
_____

❑ _____
_____
_____

❑ _____
_____
_____

❑ _____
_____
_____

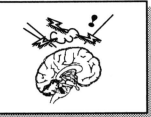

YOUR BRAINSTORMS …

Use the scenario at the beginning of this chapter or a similar problem scenario you have encountered to solve this problem and develop an action plan.

1 **Possible Quick-Recovery Solutions to the Problem**

_____

_____

_____

2 **Possible Next-Step Solutions**

_____

_____

_____

3 **Possible Long-Term Solutions**

_____

_____

_____

Rank Order the Solutions Within Each Classification

1	**2**	**3**
"QUICK RECOVERY"	**"NEXT STEP"**	**"LONG TERM"**
1._____	1._____	1._____
_____	_____	_____
_____	_____	_____
2._____	2._____	2._____
_____	_____	_____
_____	_____	_____
3._____	3._____	3._____
_____	_____	_____
_____	_____	_____

Explain *why* you ranked each solution first.

1 **Quick-Recovery Solution**

_____

_____

_____

2 **Next-Step Solution**

_____

_____

_____

3 **Long-Term Solution**

_____

_____

_____

Sequence the steps you will take to help solve this problem.

Step 1

Step 2

Step 3

Step 4

Step 5

Step 6

 SKYLIGHT PUBLISHING, INC.

Assess the effectiveness of your action plan:

_____
_____
_____
_____
_____

How will you celebrate your success?:

_____
_____
_____
_____

Reflect on a similar behavior problem you have had, review how you handled the problem at the time, and speculate about what you would do differently if you encounter the same problem again.

Problem:

_____
_____
_____
_____

What you did:

_____
_____
_____
_____

What you would do in the future:

_____
_____
_____
_____

SKYLIGHT PUBLISHING, INC.

What to Do With the Class Who ...

When All the Kids Misbehave

C*lass, class,"* yells Mrs. Paul. *"Please get back in your seats so I can give you your assignment!"*

"Bruce took my pencil," Robin whines. *"Make him give it back!"*

"In your face," mumbles Bruce.

"Students, I have a wonderful cooperative activity planned for today, but we can't start until you are all settled."

"Dave is sitting in the wrong seat," Julie announces to the class. *"Make him move!"*

"John, quit sharpening your pencil and sit down!" Mrs. Paul pleads. *"We really need to begin."*

Suddenly Kim and Terry begin to giggle uncontrollably.

"Look at Jamie's haircut," they howl. *"It looks like his mother put a bowl over his head."*

"Okay, everyone. I think we need to put away our math books and call a class meeting. We have a lot to discuss."

Sound familiar? Who has not experienced a class where "controlled chaos" is the order of the day?

In the traditional classroom, teachers might utilize the obedience model and punish the whole class by revoking a privilege ("Okay, we won't be going on our field trip to the zoo on Friday") or by threatening ("That's it—if I hear one more word the whole class will have to diagram all fifty sentences tonight for homework"). Teachers also sometimes resort to subtle forms of punishment like, "Okay class, I see we are not mature enough to handle group work today. Let's separate our desks, take out our ditto packets, and answer all the even problems! The packets must be turned in before you go home."

A more effective way to handle whole-class disruptions, however, is to hold a class meeting to discuss what the problems are, brainstorm solutions, redefine or reset rules as needed, set class goals, and build consensus.

Class Meeting

"Class, I've called this meeting so that we can discuss what just happened in our math class," Mrs. Paul begins.

"You mean, because we all were bad?" offers Robin.

"I mean when we were not treating each other with respect," replies Mrs. Paul. *"What do you think we can do about it?"*

"Well," Lisa offers. *"We could review our social skills."*

"What do you mean?" asks Julie.

"Well, I think we could review 'put-downs,' " says John.

"You mean like 'in your face'?" Bruce asks.

"Yeah," replies John. *"We could practice getting into groups, taking turns, and giving each other encouragement."*

"We used to encourage all the time," Jamie adds.

"That's true." Julie answers.

"Okay, so what can we do?" asks Dave.

"I know," exclaims Terry. *" We can do another T-chart on what cooperation looks like and sounds like."*

"Good idea," says Michelle. *"And then we can role play 'put-downs' and how they make us feel."*

"Okay, that's fine," says Robin. *"But how are we going to keep track of who is still using put-downs and who is using put-ups?"*

"We can use checklists in our groups to keep track of put-downs," says Dave.

"What will we get if we go a whole day without slamming someone?" asks Bruce. *"A happy face?"*

"No," says Robin. *"We'll give each other a round of applause when the bell rings."*

"Let me summarize what you have all suggested and then we can have a class vote to decide on the ideas," offers Mrs. Paul.

"Terry, please write the following on the board:"

1. Get into base groups and complete T-charts on social skills we feel we need.
2. Use checklists to monitor our own behavior and the behavior of our base group members.
3. Encourage each other by giving the group a round of applause at the end of the day if we all practice our targeted social skills.

"Beth, will you please conduct the discussion on each of the three proposals?"

"Okay, all those in favor of proposal one will have a chance to discuss their views. And then anyone opposed will also be able to state their opposition or offer alternative proposals. Discussion for each proposal will be limited to five minutes. Remember to 'disagree with the idea—not the person.'"

(Discussion for all three proposals lasts 15 minutes.)

"Thank you, Beth. You did a good job conducting the discussion. I think we are now ready to take a reading using 'five-to-fist'," says Mrs. Paul.

(Class takes a reading.)

"Well class, I am pleased that we came to consensus and arrived at some procedures we can all live with. I am also anxious to see how your behavior checklists work. Usually I am the one who monitors your behavior, but now you have accepted the responsibility to monitor yourselves. I respect your desire to work together to solve your problems. Let's give ourselves a standing ovation for working so well together," Mrs. Paul announces.

"And now let's review a T-chart on cooperation as a class before we brainstorm the social skills we all feel we need to review. . . ."

T-Chart
Cooperation

What does it look like?	What does it sound like?
working together	"I like that idea."
helping one another	"Do you need any help?"
smiling	"Thanks for helping me."
sharing	"Way to go!"
eye to eye	"I like working with you."
knee to knee	"That's a great idea!"

Students need to review the classroom procedures, rules, consequences, and the cooperative group rules and social skills on a periodic basis. It would be naive to assume that teaching the social skills once in September is enough to embed them firmly in the students' minds until June.

FOCUS STRATEGY:
Group Observation Checklist for Social Skills

Strategy

Directions:
1. Select two target social skills you plan to observe for one activity, one day, or one week.
2. Put a "✓" every time you observe your team members use the social skill.
3. Fill in the comment section below.
4. Share your observations and comments with group members.

Date: *First Semester*

Class: *Math*

Teacher: *Mrs. Paul*

GROUP MEMBERS	TARGETED SOCIAL SKILLS	MON.	TUES.	WED.	THURS.	FRI.	TOTAL
1. Jeff	a. encouraging	✓					1
	b. paraphrasing	✓✓	✓✓	✓✓	✓✓	✓✓	10
2. Terry	a. encouraging	✓✓	✓✓✓	✓✓✓	✓✓	✓✓	12
	b. paraphrasing	✓	✓	✓✓	✓	✓	6
3. Carol	a. encouraging		✓				1
	b. paraphrasing	✓✓	✓✓	✓✓		✓	7

Comments about Members

1. Jeff: <u>You are a good listener because you always report or paraphrase what people</u> <u>say. However, you hardly ever encourage. You tend to "put down" people rather</u> <u>than build them up.</u>

2. Terry: <u>You really keep the group going by both listening and energizing them. You're</u> <u>a group cheerleader.</u>

3. Carol: <u>You give few positive comments to anyone, although you do listen well.</u>

Group Member Observer: *Pat*   Date: *Sept. 9*

Behavior Checklists

In addition to the T-chart and student-initiated behavior checklists, teachers might want to use behavior checklists to monitor appropriate classroom behavior to get a feel for where the "breakdown" of rules is occurring. Several types of observation checklists can be used to monitor areas that the whole class needs help with or areas where specific students are weak. The checklists can also be used as documentation for school referrals or parent conferences.

FOCUS STRATEGY:
Group Behavior Checklist

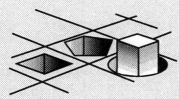
Strategy

Record observed use of social skills by writing the date they occurred in the appropriate column. "Catch them being good!"

Dates _Second Semester_

Class: _Reading_

Teacher: _Mrs. Brown_

Assessment of Social Skills

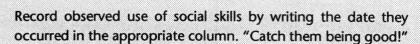

Who	Skill 1 Using 12" Voices	Skill 2 Taking Turns	Skill 3 Listening to Others	Skill 4 Reaching Consensus	Skill 5 Helping Each Other	Celebrations
1. Terry	$^{10}/_1$, $^{11}/_3$, $^{12}/_6$					
2. Jeff						
3. Mike				$^{11}/_2$, $^6/_1$	$^{11}/_5$, $^{12}/_6$, $^{12}/_{15}$	all-class hurrah
4. Pat						
5. Carol	$^{10}/_1$, $^{10}/_3$, $^{10}/_4$					
6. Lois						
7. Mary Lou						
8. George						
9. Jane			$^6/_1$, $^6/_3$, $^6/_5$			
10. Ed	$^{10}/_2$	$^{11}/_5$, $^{11}/_6$, $^{11}/_7$	$^{11}/_6$, $^{11}/_7$			note from me
11. Thomas						
12. Donna						
13. Bruce						
14. Colleen						
15. Dan		$^{12}/_3$, $^1/_6$, $^2/_4$	$^2/_6$, $^2/_9$			round of applause
16. Kathy						
17. Bobby						
18. Danny						
19. E.J.					$^{10}/_1$, $^{10}/_5$	
20. Lucy						

Behavior checklists provide concrete documentation at a glance. Some teachers prefer to "check" whenever they witness the behavior occurring in the student. Any blanks on the checklists would, therefore, indicate a deficiency in the student's behavior.

Other teachers find it less time consuming and more efficient to document only those students who are having problems. By focusing on the target behaviors and the student who has problems, the teacher can address those specific behaviors immediately, early in the year, or whenever a series of violations occurs.

GROUP BEHAVIOR CHECKLIST

Target social skill: _Not interrupting others_

Check (✔) the number of times each person interrupts when another person is talking.

Group members	M	T	W	T	F
Patsy	✔ ✔ ✔	✔ ✔ ✔	✔ ✔ ✔	✔ ✔	✔
Tom	✔ ✔	✔	✔		
Karen		✔	✔		
Joe	✔	✔			

Self-Evaluation (How did you do?): _I think I might have a problem. I never realized how much I interrupted when other people were talking. I've got to control my outbursts._

Group Evaluation (How did your group do?): _Overall, my group did pretty well. Tom tends to interrupt too much, but Karen and Joe are good listeners._

Signed: _Patsy_   Date: _9/27/92_

If a teacher notices that many of the students are violating one or more of the rules or social skills, it is time to take "class action" by addressing the problem as a whole group rather than addressing the problem individually with the student who repeatedly violates the rule.

The Behavior Checklists can also be used by cooperative groups to monitor their group behavior. They can fill in the targeted behaviors in the columns and assess how they did individually and as a group after each activity, at the end of each day, or at the end of the week. By taking time to process their own behaviors, students in a group can reflect on the importance of practicing social skills and learn how to achieve academic goals by learning how to interact effectively with others.

Conclusion

The role of the teacher is changing. Glasser says that teachers must see themselves as "modern managers" whose roles go far beyond the traditional concept of directing, rewarding, and punishing students.

> *Unlike traditional managers who spend little time worrying about whether the working conditions are satisfying, modern managers spend a lot of time structuring and restructuring the workplace to make it more satisfying because they believe that satisfied workers [students] are much more productive.* (Glasser, 1986, p. 81)

Traditional managers rely on power to threaten students, give them detentions, call their parents, get them suspended, get them expelled, or fail them. Despite the arsenal of punitive alternatives available, at least half of the students still will not work. The stimulus-response theory does not work with kids. Glasser (1986) notes that since most teachers fell into the "satisfied working half" of students when they were in school, "they believe in punishment because they 'remember' that it frightened them" (p. 82). He continues that when those who did not work were punished, they usually dropped out of school and no one missed them. Today, however, despite the stimuli of threats and punishment, many of the "non-working" students stay in school because "their friends are there."

The modern managers in today's classroom must meet the needs of *all* of their students. They must act as facilitators, encouragers, support and resource people, and, most importantly, managers of cooperative learning teams.

271

The most difficult task for teachers who are trying to learn to manage learning-teams is to understand the difference between a modern manager, who is willing to share power and is always on the lookout for better ways to do this, and a traditional manager, who never willingly gives up any power and is always looking for more. (Glasser, 1986, pp. 82-83)

The quintessential manager orchestrates his or her cooperative classroom so that all of the students feel comfortable in their environment, feel "satisfied" with what they are learning, and feel they are a part of a small group and a whole class where everyone is working toward a common goal.

No one functions to full potential all the time, and lapses in the performance of social skills can jeopardize the entire group. The proactive manager is able to sense the problem before it escalates and diffuse it by using a repertoire of problem-solving techniques. Despite concentrated efforts, some "minor" problems do, in fact, become serious disturbances that must be handled quickly and effectively to preserve the nurturing classroom climate. There are no easy answers or solutions to the problems that face the manager. Just when a teacher manages to handle one discipline problem effectively, another one emerges. But if teachers apply the principles of positive classroom discipline and cooperative learning to their students, they won't have to wait until Christmas to smile—they and their students can smile every day of the school year!

BLACKLINES

BLANK PROCEDURES FORM

Grade Level _____   Subject Area _____

Procedures

A. Beginning the Class

❏ _____
❏ _____
❏ _____
❏ _____
❏ _____
❏ _____

B. Classroom Management

❏ _____
❏ _____
❏ _____
❏ _____
❏ _____
❏ _____

C. Paper Work

❏ _____
❏ _____
❏ _____
❏ _____
❏ _____
❏ _____

D. Dismissal from Class or School

❏ _____
❏ _____
❏ _____
❏ _____
❏ _____
❏ _____

E. Syllabus or Course Outline

❑ _____
❑ _____
❑ _____
❑ _____
❑ _____
❑ _____

F. Bringing Books, Notebooks, and Supplies to Class

❑ _____
❑ _____
❑ _____
❑ _____
❑ _____
❑ _____

G. Other Procedures

❑ _____
❑ _____
❑ _____
❑ _____
❑ _____
❑ _____

SKYLIGHT PUBLISHING

Classroom Rules and Consequences

Teacher: _____   Class: _____   Date: _____

Rule #1: _____

        Consequences   1. _____
                             2. _____
                             3. _____
                             4. _____
                             5. _____

Rule #2: _____

        Consequences   1. _____
                             2. _____
                             3. _____
                             4. _____
                             5. _____

Rule #3: _____

        Consequences   1. _____
                             2. _____
                             3. _____
                             4. _____
                             5. _____

Rule #4: _____

        Consequences   1. _____
                             2. _____
                             3. _____
                             4. _____
                             5. _____

Rule #5: _____

        Consequences   1. _____
                             2. _____
                             3. _____
                             4. _____
                             5. _____

Behavior Checklist

Teacher: _____   Class: _____   Date: _____

Write the date of each violation under the rule that the student violated.

Class Roll

Names	Rule 1	Rule 2	Rule 3	Rule 4	Rule 5
1. _____					
2. _____					
3. _____					
4. _____					
5. _____					
6. _____					
7. _____					
8. _____					
9. _____					
10. _____					
11. _____					
12. _____					
13. _____					
14. _____					
15. _____					
16. _____					
17. _____					
18. _____					
19. _____					
20. _____					
21. _____					
22. _____					
23. _____					
24. _____					
25. _____					
26. _____					
27. _____					
28. _____					
29. _____					
30. _____					

SKYLIGHT PUBLISHING

Discipline Checklist

Class: _____ Teacher: _____ Date:_____

Rules: Consequences:

Rule #1 _____   1. _____

Rule #2 _____   2. _____

Rule #3 _____   3. _____

Rule #4 _____   4. _____

Rule #5 _____   5. _____

Write the dates of all violations in boxes under rule numbers.

Class Roll	Rule					Comments
	1	2	3	4	5	
1.						
2.						
3.						
4.						
5.						
6.						
7.						
8.						
9.						
10.						
11.						
12.						
13.						
14.						
15.						
16.						
17.						
18.						
19.						
20.						

Burke's "Dirty Dozen"
Teacher Behaviors that Can Erode the Classroom Climate

1. **Sarcasm**   Students' feelings can be hurt by sarcastic put-downs thinly disguised as "humor."

2. **Negative Tone of Voice**   Students can "read between the lines" and sense a sarcastic, negative, or condescending tone of voice.

3. **Negative Body Language**   Clenched fists, a set jaw, a quizzical look, or standing over a student in a threatening manner can speak more loudly than any words.

4. **Inconsistency**   Nothing escapes the students' attention. They will be the first to realize the teacher is not enforcing the rules consistently.

5. **Favoritism**   "Brown-nosing" is an art and any student in any class can point out the "teacher's pet" who gets special treatment. There are no secrets in a class!

6. **Put-Downs**   Sometimes teachers are not aware they are embarrassing a student with subtle put-downs, but if teachers expect students to encourage rather than put down, they need to model positive behavior.

7. **Outbursts**   Teachers are sometimes provoked by students and they "lose it." These teacher outbursts set a bad example for the students, create a negative climate, and could lead to more serious problems.

8. **Public Reprimands**   No one wants to be corrected or humiliated in front of his peers. One way to make an enemy out of a student is to make him or her lose face in front of the other students.

9. **Unfairness**   Taking away promised privileges or rewards; scheduling a surprise test; "nitpicking" while grading homework or tests; or assigning punitive home-work could be construed by students as being "unfair."

10. **Apathy**   Students want teachers to listen to them, show them they are important, and empathize with them. If teachers convey the attitude that teaching is just a job and students are just aggravations that must be dealt with, students will respond accordingly.

11. **Inflexibility**   Some students may need extra help or special treatment in order to suc-ceed. A teacher should be flexible enough to "bend the rules" or adjust the standards to meet students' individual needs.

12. **Lack of Humor**   Teachers who cannot laugh at themselves usually have problems motiva-ting students to learn, and usually have boring classes.

SKYLIGHT PUBLISHING

SOCIAL SKILLS
Basic Interaction

Form Groups Quietly

Sit Eyeball to Eyeball

Make Eye Contact

Use Each Other's Names

Share Materials

Follow Role Assignments

T-CHART

Looks Like	**Sounds Like**

[Chapter 5, Communication Skills, p. 60]
[Chapter 22, Students with Learning Challenges, p. 225]
[Chapter 25, Students with Language Challenges, p. 250]

©1992 Skylight Publishing

SKYLIGHT PUBLISHING

SOCIAL SKILLS
Communication

Use Low Voices

Take Turns

Make Sure Everyone Has a Turn to Speak

Listen to the Speaker

Wait Until Speaker is Finished Before You Speak

VENN

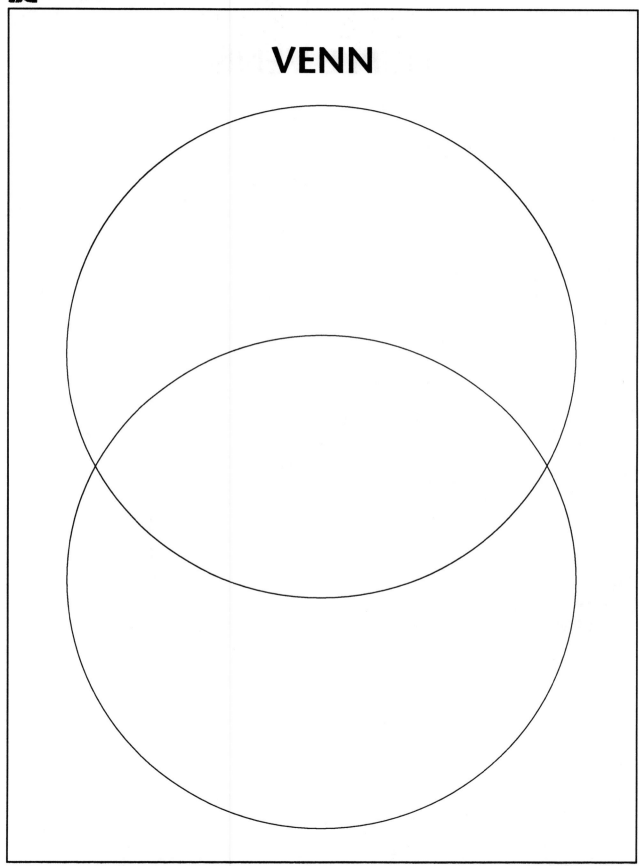

TRIPLE VENN

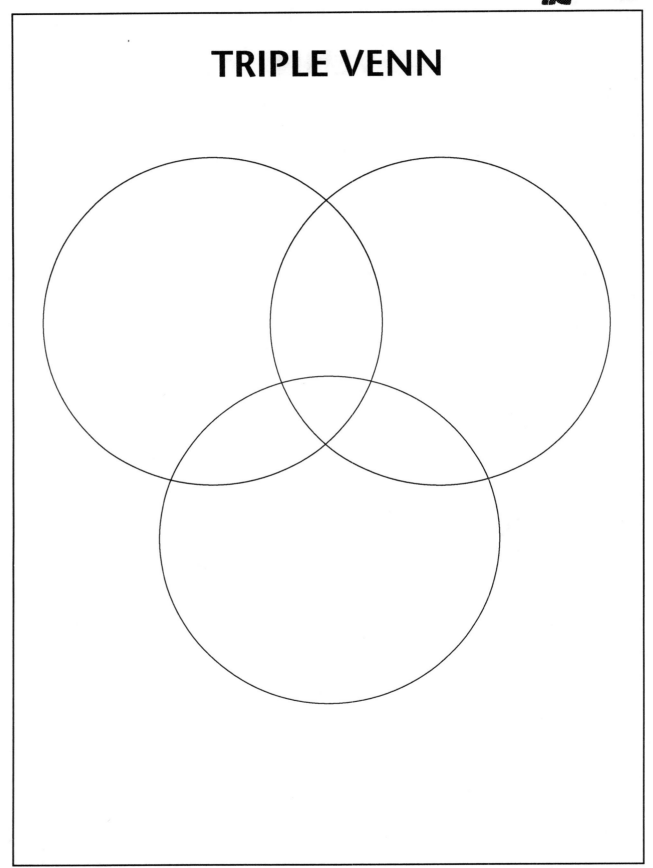

SOCIAL SKILLS
Team-Building Skills

Check for Understanding

Offer Your Help

Ask Your Group First for Help if You Don't Understand

Encourage Each Other

Energize the Group

Disagree with the Idea—Not the Person

Agree/Disagree Chart

Statement	Before		After	
	Agree	Disagree	Agree	Disagree
1.				
2.				
3.				
4.				
5.				
6.				
7.				
8.				

From *Patterns for Thinking: Patterns for Transfer* by Robin Fogarty and James Bellanca, Skylight Publishing, Palatine, IL, 1987.)

SOCIAL SKILLS

Conflict Resolution

Disagree with the Idea—Not the Person

Respect the Opinion of Others

Think for Yourself

Explore Different Points of View

Negotiate and/or Compromise

Reach Consensus

Problem-Solving Model

Student: _____ Date: _____

Teacher: _____

Student's Statement of the Problem:

_____

_____

Teacher's Statement of the Problem:

_____

_____

Student's Solutions to the Problem:

1._____

2. _____

3. _____

4. _____

5. _____

Rank Order Top Three Solutions:

1._____

2. _____

3. _____

Discuss Why Solution Number One is the Best Choice:

_____

_____

Plan of Action:

_____

_____

Time Line:

_____

Next Meeting: _____

Signature of Student: _____

Signature of Teacher: _____

Signature of Parent: _____

Phone Conference with Parent:

_____

_____

_____

_____

Assignment & Test Sheet

Assignments	Course	Due Date	Done
1.			
2.			
3.			
4.			
5.			
6.			
7.			
8.			
9.			
10.			
11.			
Tests and Quizzes	**Course**	**Date**	**Grade**
1.			
2.			
3.			
4.			
5.			
6.			
7.			
8.			
9.			
10.			
11.			

Problem-Solving Model

Student: _____   Date: _____

Teacher: _____   Problem: _____

Describe the Incident:

_____

_____

_____

Probe for Causes of Behavior:

_____

_____

_____

Brainstorm Possible Solutions to the Problem:

1. _____

2. _____

3. _____

4. _____

5. _____

List Top Three Solutions:

1. _____

2. _____

3. _____

Establish Time Line: **Date:**

1. _____   _____

2. _____   _____

3. _____   _____

Follow-up Meeting: _____

Signature of Student: _____

Signature of Teacher: _____

Decision-Making Model

Start
↓

WHAT IS THE DILEMMA?

ALTERNATIVES

CONSEQUENCES

+	+	+	+
−	−	−	−

DECISION

Student: _____ Teacher: _____ Date: _____

Problem: _____

_____

Final Decision: _____

_____

Follow-up meeting: _____

[Chapter 11, Students Who Are Off Task, p. 119]

©1992 Skylight Publishing

Telegram

TELEGRAM ═══════════

Dateline: _____

To: _____

From: _____

Social Contract

Student: _____ Date: _____

Teacher: _____

Teacher: Describe the problem.

_____

_____

_____

Student: What is your reaction to the problem your teacher has described?

_____

_____

_____

Teacher and Student: Decide on a Social Contract to help solve the problem.

Steps taken by the teacher
1._____
2._____
3._____
4._____

Steps taken by the student
1._____
2._____
3._____
4._____

Positive consequences of fulfilling the Social Contract:
1._____
2. _____
3. _____

Negative consequences of **not** fulfilling the Social Contract:
1._____
2. _____
3. _____

Timeline for the contract: _____

When and where we meet again to discuss the results of the Social Contract:

Place: _____ Student's Signature _____ Date: _____

Time: _____ Teacher's Signature _____ Date: _____

Date: _____ Parent's Signature _____ Date: _____

SKYLIGHT PUBLISHING

Decision-Making Model

Student: _____ Date: _____ Teacher: _____

Problem

Alternative Solutions

Pros and Cons

Solution #1

Pro

Con

Solution #2

Pro

Con

Solution #3

Pro

Con

Final Decision

Reasons

Cause-and-Effect Model

Student: _____ Date: _____ Teacher: _____

Specific Behavior   **Effect It Could Have on Others**

Reflection on Behaviors: _____

_____

_____

Targeted Behavior to Change: _____

_____

Signed: _____   Date: _____

Group Social Contract

Group members: _____

Date: _____

Problem: _____

Each person's statement of what he or she can do to help solve the problem:

1: _____

_____

2: _____

_____

3: _____

_____

4: _____

_____

Timeline: _____

Next meeting: _____

Goal: _____

How will we celebrate success: _____

_____

Signed: _____   _____

   _____   _____

Newspaper Model

Name: _____   Date: _____

Problem: _____

Who	What	When	Where	Why

Write a paragraph commenting on the situation you have described above.

Have another group member write a paragraph about the situation.

SKYLIGHT PUBLISHING

Phases of a Power Struggle

Analyze the power struggle to determine what proactive things could have been done to prevent the explosion, what things escalated the problem, how the problem erupted, what steps were taken to diffuse tempers, and possible resolutions to the power play.

Explosion Effect

Causes

Build up

Cool down

Diffuse Temper

Prevention

What could have been done to prevent the problem?

Resolution

Ways to resolve problem

(Used with permission from Bob Wiedmann, The IRI Group)

Reflective Divided Journal

Name: _____

Date: _____

Description of Action

Signed: _____

Name: _____

Date: _____

Upon Reflection

Signed: _____

Behavior Observation Checklist

Student: _____ Date: _____

Behavior	Mon.	Tues.	Wed.	Thurs.	Fri.	Total
TOTAL						

What day do you have the *fewest* behavior problems? _____

Why do you think you are better on that day? _____

_____

What day do you have the *most* behavior problems? _____

Why do you think you behave poorly on that day? _____

_____

What negative behavior do you use the most? _____

Why? _____

What can you do to improve your behavior? _____

_____

Weekly Behavior Log

Name: _____ Targeted Behavior: _____

Date: _____ Incident: _____
_____
_____

Date: _____ Incident: _____
_____
_____

Date: _____ Incident: _____
_____
_____

Date: _____ Incident: _____
_____
_____

Date: _____ Incident: _____
_____
_____

Reflection on Week: _____
_____
_____
_____

Plan for Next Week: _____
_____
_____
_____

Specific Things I Can Try: _____
_____
_____
_____
_____
_____
_____
_____

SKYLIGHT PUBLISHING

Modified Case Study

Student: _____   School: _____

Teacher: _____   Date: _____   Age: _____

Briefly describe the problem the student is having in class

_____

_____

_____

Log of specific behavior

_____

_____

_____

_____

_____

_____

Pertinent information from permanent files

_____

_____

_____

Test scores

_____

_____

Contact with parent

_____

_____

_____

Contact with counselor or administrator (ask about evaluations done by school psychologists or sociologists)

_____

_____

_____

Conference with student

_____

_____

_____

Follow-up meeting

_____

K–W–L

Name of Student:
Date:
Title of Unit:

K What I Know	**W** What I Want to Know	**L** What I've Learned

Research Task:

Project:

Due Date:

Reflection:

Signed:

Ranking

Student: _____ Team: _____ Date: _____

List your strengths in any area (writing, art, music, speaking, organization, cooking, etc.)

• Discuss your strengths with your fellow group members.

• File lists in your team notebook and review them before discussing team projects.

• Update individual lists as new talents or strengths emerge.

• Draw on the strengths of each team member when developing group projects.

Group Observation Checklist

Group Observation Checklist
for Social Skills

Dates _____

Class: _____

Teacher: _____

Directions:
1. Select two target social skills you plan to observe for one activity, one day, or one week.
2. Put a "✓" every time you observe your team members use the social skill.
3. Fill in the comment section below.
4. Share your observations and comments with group members.

GROUP MEMBERS	TARGETED SOCIAL SKILLS	MON.	TUES.	WED.	THURS.	FRI.	TOTAL
1.	a.						
	b.						
2.	a.						
	b.						
3.	a.						
	b.						
4.	a.						
	b.						

Comments

_____

_____

_____

_____

_____

_____

_____

_____

Signed: _____ Date: _____

[Epilogue, When All the Kids Misbehave, p. 266]

Group Behavior Checklist

Assessment of Social Skills						
Dates: _____ Class:_____ Teacher:_____						
Who	Skill 1	Skill 2	Skill 3	Skill 4	Skill 5	Celebrations
1.						
2.						
3.						
4.						
5.						
6.						
7.						
8.						
9.						
10.						
11.						
12.						
13.						
14.						
15.						
16.						
17.						
18.						
19.						
20.						

GROUP BEHAVIOR CHECKLIST

Target social skill: _____

Group members	**M**	**T**	**W**	**T**	**F**

Self-Evaluation (How did you do?): _____
_____
_____
_____
_____

Group Evaluation (How did your group do?): _____
_____
_____
_____
_____

Signed: _____ **Date:** _____

[Epilogue, When All the Kids Misbehave, p. 268]

Bibliography

Arias, M. B. (1983). *Teacher and student behaviors in contrasting bilingual settings.* Paper presented at the American Education Research Association meeting, Montreal.

Banks, J. A. (1991, December). Multicultural education for freedom's sake. *Educational Leadership, 49*(4), 32-36.

Barclay, J. R., & Kehle, T. J. (1979). The impact of handicapped students on other students in the classroom. *Journal of Research and Development in Education, 12*(4).

Bellanca, J. (1991). *Building a caring, cooperative classroom: A social skills primer.* Palatine, IL: Skylight Publishing.

Bellanca, J., & Fogarty, R. (1991). *Blueprints for thinking in the cooperative classroom.* Palatine, IL: Skylight Publishing.

Board of Education for the City of Etobicoke Writing Committee. (1987). *Making the grade: Evaluating student progress.* Scarborough, Ontario: Prentice-Hall Canada, Inc.

Borba, M. (1990). *Improving student achievement and behavior through self-esteem.* Palm Springs, CA: Author.

Borba, M. (1989). *Esteem builders: A self-esteem curriculum for improving student achievement, behavior, and school-home climate.* Rolling Hills Estates, CA: Jalmar Press.

Borba, M., & Borba, C. (1982). *Self-esteem: A classroom affair, Vol. II.* San Francisco: Harper Collins Publishers.

Borba, M., & Borba, C. (1978). *Self-esteem: A classroom affair—101 ways to help children like themselves.* San Francisco: HarperCollins Publishers.

Brandt, R. (March, 1988). On students' needs and team learning: A conversation with William Glasser. *Educational Leadership, 45*(6), 38-45.

Brantigan, N. S., McElliott, K. (1991). *Creating a quality-based school: A model for the 21st century.* Paper presented at the National Middle School Association Conference, Louisville, Kentucky, Nov. 8-11, 1991.

Chapman, S. (1991, September 22). "Real and false solutions for teen pregnancies." *Chicago Tribune*, Section 4, p. 3.

Chernow, F. B., & Chernow, C. (1981). *Classroom discipline and control: 101 practical techniques.* West Nyack, NY: Parker Publishing Company, Inc.

Cohen, E. G. (1991, October). Strategies for creating a multi-ability classroom. *Cooperative Learning, 12*(1).

Cohen, E. G. (1986). *Designing groupwork: Strategies for the heterogeneous classroom.* New York: Teachers College Press.

Collis, M., & Dalton, J. (1990). *Becoming responsible learners: Strategies for positive classroom management.* Portsmouth, NH: Heinemann Educational Books, Inc.

Crary, E. (1984). *Kids can cooperate: A practical guide to teaching problem solving.* Seattle: Parenting Press, Inc.

Curry, G. (1991, October 9). "Experts rethink effect violence has on kids." *Chicago Tribune*, Section 1A, p. 23.

Curwin, R. L., & Mendler, A. N. (1988). *Discipline with dignity.* Alexandria, VA: Association for Supervision and Curriculum Development.

Dinkmeyer, D. & Losoncy, L. E. (1980). *The encouragement book: Becoming a positive person.* New York: Prentice-Hall Press.

Dinkmeyer, D., McKay, G. D., & Dinkmeyer, D., Jr. (1980). *Systematic training for effective teaching.* Circle Pines, MN: American Guidance Service, Inc.

Dreikurs, R., Grunwald, B., & Pepper, F. (1980). *Maintaining sanity in the classroom.* (2nd ed.). New York: Harper & Row.

Educational Programs Department. (1989). *Year 2000: A framework for learning.* Victoria, B.C.: Ministry of Education.

Eitzen, D. S. (1992, April). Problem students: The sociocultural roots. *Phi Delta Kappan, 73*(8), 584-590.

Evertson, C., & Harris, A. (1992, April). What we know about managing classrooms: Synthesis of research. *Educational Leadership, 49*(7), 74-78.

Evertson, C., & Harris, A. (1991a). *Classroom organization and management program: Selected excerpts from workshop manual for elementary teachers.* Nashville, TN: Vanderbilt University.

Evertson, C., & Harris, A. (1991b). *Components of effective classroom management: Materials selected from the NDN-approved classroom organization and management program (COMP)*. Nashville, TN: Vanderbilt University.

Executive Committee of the Council for Children with Behavioral Disorders. (May, 1989). Position statement on the Regular Education Initiative. *Behavioral Disorders, 14*(3), 201-207.

Gage, N. L. (1990, December). Dealing with the dropout problem. *Phi Delta Kappan, 72*(4), 280-285.

Glasser, W. (1990). *The quality school.* New York: Harper Perennial.

Glasser, W. (1986). *Control theory in the classroom.* New York: Harper & Row.

Goodlad, J. I. (1984). *A place called school: Prospects for the future.* New York: McGraw-Hill.

Gordon, T. (1974). *Teacher effectiveness training.* New York: Peter Wyden.

Gough, P. B. (1987, May). The key to improving schools: An interview with William Glasser. *Phi Delta Kappan, 68*(9), 657.

Hanson, P. (1966). *What is feedback?* (Participant's notebook). Houston: Human Relations Training Laboratory, VA Hospital.

Hatch, E. M. (1977). *An historical overview of second language acquisition research.* Paper presented at the First Annual Second Language Research Forum, University of California at Los Angeles.

Hill, D. (1990, April). Order in the classroom. *Teacher Magazine, 1*(7), 70-77.

Hodgkinson, H. (1991, September). Reform versus reality. *Phi Delta Kappan, 73*(1), 9-16.

Jenkins, P. (1989). *The joyful child: A sourcebook of activities and ideas for releasing children's natural joy.* Tucson, AZ: Harbinger House, Inc.

Johnson, D. W., Johnson, R. T., & Holubec, E. J. (1988). *Cooperation in the classroom.* Edina, MN: Interaction Book Company.

Kendall, P. (1990, October 29). "Dropout tendency starts with ABCs." *Chicago Tribune,* Section 2, p. 1.

Kohn, A. (1991, March). Caring kids: The role of the schools. *Phi Delta Kappan, 72*(7), 496-506.

Kounin, & Gump. (1992). In Everston, C., & Harris, A. (1992, April). What we know about managing classrooms: Synthesis of research. *Educational Leadership, 49* (7), 74-78.

Krashen, S. (1981). Bilingual education and second language acquisition theory. In M. Ortiz, D. Parker, & S. F. Tempes (Eds.), *Schooling and language minority students: A theoretical framework.* Sacramento, CA: Office of Bilingual Education. Department of Education, 125-134.

McDaniel, T. R. (1986). A primer on classroom discipline: Principles old and new. *Phi Delta Kappan, 68*(1), 64.

McKay, G. W. (1976). *The basics of encouragement.* Coral Springs, FL: CMTI Press.

Neves, A. (1983). *The effect of various input on the second language acquisition of Mexican American children in nine elementary school classrooms.* Unpublished doctoral dissertation, Stanford University.

Oakes, J. (1985). *Keeping track: How schools structure equality.* New Haven, CT: Yale University Press.

Page, C. (1992, March 8). "Reading and writing reality." *Chicago Tribune,* Section 4, p. 3.

Purkey, W. (1971). *Self-concepts and school achievement.* Englewood Cliffs, NJ: Prentice-Hall.

Sapon-Shevin, M. (1991, October). Cooperative learning in inclusive classrooms: Learning to become a community. *Cooperative Learning, 12*(1), 8-9.

Sullivan, B. (1991, September 22). "Is a nation of children being neglected?" *Chicago Tribune,* Section 6, p. 5.

Tateyama-Sniezek, K. (1990). Cooperative learning: Does it improve the academic achievement of students with handicaps? *Exceptional Children, 56*(5), 426-437.

Taylor, A. R., Asher, S. R., Williams, G. A. (1986). *Loneliness, goal orientation, and socio-metric status: Mildly retarded children's adaptation to the mainstream classroom.* Paper presented at the annual meeting of the American Educational Research Association, San Francisco.

Wang, M. C., & Reynolds, M. C. (1985). Avoiding the "Catch-22" in special education reform. *Exceptional Children, 51*(6), 487-495.

Warshaw, M. (1986, September). Return from the tower. *Phi Delta Kappan, 68*(1), 67-69.

Will, M. (1986). *Educating students with learning problems: A shared responsibility.* Washington, DC: U. S. Department of Education.

Index

W

Y

Notes

Notes

Learn from Our Books *and* from Our Authors!

Bring Our Author/Trainers to Your District

At IRI/Skylight, we have assembled a unique team of outstanding author/trainers with international reputations for quality work. Each has designed high-impact programs that translate powerful new research into successful learning strategies for every student. We design each program to fit your school's or district's special needs.

1 Training Programs

Gain practical techniques and strategies for implementing the latest findings from educational research. IRI/Skylight is recognized around the world for its commitment to translating cognitive and cooperative learning research into high-quality resource materials and effective classroom practices. In each program IRI/Skylight designs, participants learn by doing the thinking and cooperating they will be asking their students to do. With IRI/Skylight's specially prepared materials, participants learn how to teach their students to learn for a lifetime.

2 Networks for Systemic Change

Through partnerships with Phi Delta Kappa and others, IRI/Skylight offers two Networks for site-based systemic change: *The Network of Mindful Schools* and *The Multiple Intelligences School Network.* The Networks are designed to promote systemic school change as practical and possible when starting with a renewed vision that centers on *what* and *how* each student learns. To help accomplish this goal, Network consultants work with member schools to develop an annual tactical plan and implement the plan at the classroom level.

3 Training of Trainers

The Training of Trainers programs train your best teachers, those who provide the highest quality instruction, to coach other teachers. This not only increases the number of teachers you can afford to train in each program, but also increases the amount of coaching and follow-up that each teacher can receive from a resident expert. Our Training of Trainers programs will help you make a systemic improvement in your staff development program.

To receive a free copy of the IRI/Skylight catalog, find out more about the Networks for Systemic Change, or receive more information about trainings offered through IRI/Skylight, contact

IRI/Skylight Training and Publishing, Inc.
2626 S. Clearbrook Dr., Arlington Heights, IL 60005

800-348-4474
FAX 847-290-6609

There are
one-story intellects,
two-story intellects, and three-story
intellects with skylights. All fact collectors, who
have no aim beyond their facts, are one-story men. Two-story men
compare, reason, generalize, using the labors of the fact collectors as
well as their own. Three-story men idealize, imagine,
predict—their best illumination comes from
above, through the skylight.
—*Oliver Wendell*
Holmes

SkyLight
TRAINING AND PUBLISHING, INC.